COLORADO

Off the Beaten Path

"Given the meticulous quality of Casewit's research, *Colorado: Off the Beaten Path* may well be the perfect guide for newcomers to our slice of the continent . . . Offers a refreshing change of pace and a delightful new vision of our state."
— KCFR Radio, Denver

"A fascinating guide that enables the reader to explore both well-trodden and little-known areas of the state. Using the book as an aid, you will discover your own Colorado, a personal version of one of America's most beautiful states."
— *The News Tribune*, Fort Pierce/Port St. Lucie, Florida

"You can do no better than to take this guide to unique places a mile high and above with you. It is well illustrated, organized, and written. An excellent companion for an exciting holiday."
— *The Counselor* newsletter, Hillsdale, N.J.

"Rocky Mountain adventurers need to know of *Colorado: Off the Beaten Path* by Curtis Casewit . . . ."
— *FYI Travel Tips*

COLORADO
Off the Beaten Path

Curtis Casewit

A Voyager Book

Chester, Connecticut 06412

Library of Congress Cataloging-in-Publication Data

Casewit, Curtis W.
  Colorado, off the beaten path.

  Includes index.
  1. Colorado—Description and travel—1981–
—Guidebooks. I. Title.
F774.3.C37   1987   917.88′0433   86-4568
ISBN 0-88742-025-7

Manufactured in the United States of America

First Edition/Second Printing, September 1987

Acknowledgments

This book was written with the help of many people. The author would like to thank Richard Grant, Denver Metro Convention and Visitors Bureau; Bill Saul, National Western Stock Show; Roi Davis, Buckhorn Exchange and Museum; Leo Goto, Wellshire Inn; Kereen Allord and Su Wright, Denver researchers; William Madsen, Public Affairs, U.S. Air Force Academy; Sigi Faller, the Broadmoor Resort; Bob and Virginia Akins, Longs Peak Inn; Bill Sageser and M. Pierce, Tamarron; Christy Metz, National Park Service; Lillian Ross, Keystone Lodge and Resort; Dave Smith, Hi Country Haus Resort; Tina Harris, Beaver Village and Preferred Properties, Winter Park; Paula Anderson, Antlers Lionshead; John Fisher and Randy George, C Lazy U Ranch; and finally, Helen Evans, my special travel companion.

Curtis Casewit

Denver, Colorado

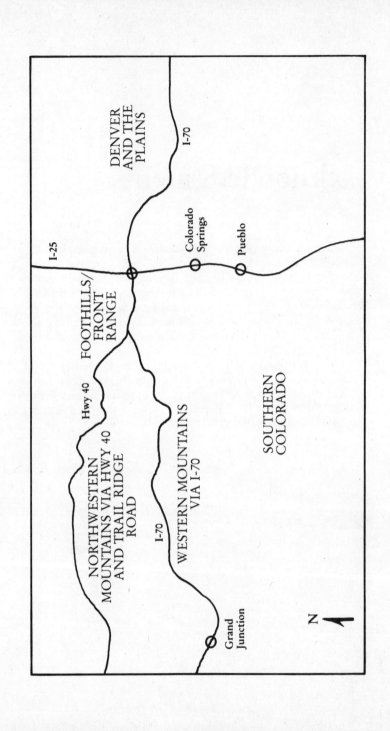

Contents

Introduction

I first saw Colorado in 1948.

It was love at first sight. I have never been able to tear myself away, despite opportunities elsewhere. The state's beauty kept me here; indeed, there followed almost 40 years of exploration. By automobile, train, plane. On foot and on horseback. On skis and on snowshoes.

From the tourist's viewpoint, Colorado has everything one could desire; travelers spend around $4 billion here each year. The state even holds surprises for natives or longtime inhabitants. Indeed, after all those years of roaming through Colorado, this book was written in a constant state of amazement.

Denver itself is packed with the unexpected. And remarkably enough, you can drive a mere 30 minutes from the state capital to reach the swish and rush of mountain streams, view dramatic rocks, or wander among thick forests. Higher and higher mountains beckon to the west; to the east, the placid plains offer new sights as well.

Colorado: Off the Beaten Path has assembled some of the state's most unique locales—some of which cannot be found in other travel books. The selections cover a wide area but are purely personal choices. Some of the attractions may be readily recognized but were visited and reviewed by this writer with a fresh slant. Many of the descriptions will be of interest to new settlers as well as those who have lived here for many decades. Naturally, suggestions for future editions are welcome.

A word about the book's organization.

Few people hereabouts know the names of counties. So each

chapter deals with a *region*. In chapter 1, for instance, you visit the foothills and front range. Chapter 2 takes you along one of Colorado's main arteries—I-70—to famous western mountains, all the way from historic Georgetown to Glenwood Springs and beyond, with one or two side trips into nearby valleys. Where to next? It was logical to explore in chapter 3 the important sights of Colorado's northwestern mountains via the important U.S. 40 and the unusual Trail Ridge Road through the magnificent Rocky Mountain National Park. Chapter 4 deals with the state's southern region including Colorado Springs. Lastly, Denver and the plains are the subjects of chapter 5. In every instance, the focus was on the uniqueness of a destination.

Finally, a word about prices. Globe Pequot Press books aim to be practical, so the reader of *Colorado: Off The Beaten Path* deserves to know what to expect. The rates for hotels and restaurants are as follows: inexpensive, moderate, expensive. A few establishments get a "deluxe" label. Most of the state's hoteliers and restaurateurs believe in good values, though.

Happy Traveling!

COLORADO

Off the Beaten Path

Colorado Foothills and Front Range

Red Rocks Park and Amphitheatre

When you come upon the 70-million-year-old **Red Rocks,** west of Denver, for the first time, the primeval scene takes your breath away: huge reddish sandstone formations jut upward and outward. Each is higher than Niagara Falls. The view conjures up dinosaurs, sea serpents and flying reptiles; indeed, tracks of these long extinct creatures have been found here, along with valuable fossil fragments. The colors are those of the Grand Canyon; one can easily believe the geologists who speak of earth-shattering monolith-building cataclysms, of retreating ancestral oceans, iron oxide color, water erosion. Geographers once called this site one of the Seven Wonders of the World.

The U.S. Geographical Survey showed up for eager surveys in 1868. By 1906, financier John Walker had acquired the land; the acoustics of these rocks would be perfect for an amphitheatre. A visiting opera singer, Dame Nellie Melba, was quick to agree; it would make one of the world's greatest open air stages. John Walker eventually donated the land to the community, and in 1927 it was incorporated into the Denver Mountain Parks System.

Construction started a few years later; dedication of the tiered outdoor area followed in 1941. The Denver Symphony soon brought its famed orchestra to the site. The latter not only produced perfect sound and aesthetic inspiration but also allowed a magnificent look at Denver far below.

During many years, the outdoor theatre experienced triumphant ballet performances, and audiences heard celebrated orchestras and even portions of Wagner operas. Singers like Lily Pons, Jennie Tourel and Helen Traubel all raved about the Red Rocks. Even the difficult-to-please Leopold Stokowski was impressed by a setting that included a "Creation Rock."

In 1959, in the interests of still further improvements, Denver's Manager of Parks flew to Germany at his own expense. He persuaded Wolfgang Wagner, grandson of the composer, to inspect Red Rocks. Wagner eventually remodeled the orchestra pit and made other design changes.

The cost of bringing large orchestras and opera companies proved to be financially difficult, however. What's more, per-

13

Chapter 1
Colorado Foothills and Front Range

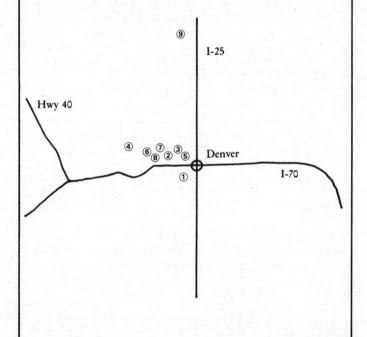

Hwy 40

I-25

Denver

I-70

1 Red Rocks
2 Buffalo Bill's Grave
3 Lookout Mountain
4 Winter Park
5 Golden-Heritage Square
6 Central City
7 Black Hawk Inn
8 St. Mary's Glacier
9 Boulder

N

Red Rocks outdoor Theatre serves music — especially rock singers

formers sometimes fought with winds that would tear away the musician's notes or with sudden five-minute rains that would drench the singers to the depth of their costumes.

Since 1961, the Red Rocks rarely heard any more classical music; instead, by the midsixties, the Beatles made a full throttle appearance here. Through the seventies and eighties, there followed assorted high-decibel rock, pop, blues, jazz and country western stars—often with sellouts of the 9,000 seats. Tickets are expensive. Fortunately, the public gets free admission at all other times. Traditionally, too, a free Easter Sunrise Service has taken place here for several decades.

The **Red Rocks Park and Amphitheatre** is easy to reach via numerous routes. From Denver, you can take West Alameda Avenue west, or drive U.S. 285 west, or follow I-70 west and watch for the marked exit. The total distance varies between 14 and 17 miles, depending on your route.

Buffalo Bill's Museum and Grave

Buffalo Bill was a unique character of the frontier. And the museum that bears his name, 12 miles west of central Denver, on Lookout Mountain, has a unique western character. Here are the mementos that bring a fascinating man to life: the paintings and posters that show him in full regalia on his white

15

horse, white of beard, cowboy hat jaunty on his head. You can see his clothes, saddles, old weapons, even a stuffed buffalo and lots of Indian artifacts.

Buffalo Bill's Museum is crammed with photographs that retrace his careers as a buffalo hunter, Indian fighter, army scout (for U.S. Army General Sheridan, among others).

Born as William F. Cody, Buffalo Bill led an extraordinary life. As a longtime Pony Express rider, he was pursued by Indians, escaping (as he wrote), "by laying flat on the back of my fast steed. I made a 24-mile straight run on one horse." On another occasion, he rode 320 miles in some 21 hours to deliver the mails. (En route, he exhausted 20 horses for the journey.) He had few rivals as a hunter and was said to have shot 4,280 bison in a 1½-year period. His slogan: "Never missed and never will/always aims and shoots to kill."

The buffalo shooting had a purpose, of course; the meat was needed to feed some 1,200 men who were laying track for the railroad. And though William Cody had his battles with the Indians, he later learned the Sioux language and befriended the Cheyennes, among other tribes.

William Cody may have had his best times as a circus rider, actor and showman, gaining fame all over the world. The first "Buffalo Bill Wild West Show" opened in 1883. The extravaganza toured for nearly three decades, spreading the myths and legends of the American West around the globe. Almost a hundred mounted Sioux Indians chased wagon trains and a stagecoach; Annie Oakley and Johnny Baker amazed audiences with their marksmanship; 83 cowboys rode bucking broncos, thereby formalizing a cowboy sport into rodeo; and the entire Battle of Little Big Horn was recreated. Spectators could see live elk and deer from Colorado. There were horse races and even a bison hunt complete with a charging herd. At its height, Buffalo Bill's show employed more than 600 performers. And in one year, he traveled 10,000 miles, performing in 132 cities in 190 days.

Cody's flowing white hair, his short white beard and rifle-holding figure symbolized the Wild West in many European capitals. Buffalo Bill gave a command performance for Queen Victoria at Windsor Castle and amused Kaiser Wilhelm II in Berlin.

Toward the end of his life, he turned into an entrepreneur and author. He gave most of his life's savings away for various good causes.

His money ran out; his fame did not.

When Buffalo Bill died, President Woodrow Wilson wired his condolences, former President Teddy Roosevelt called Cody "an American of Americans." The Colorado legislature passed a special resolution ordering that his body lay in state under the gold-plated rotunda of the State Capitol in Denver. Nearly 25,000 people turned out to pay their last respects and march in his funeral on Memorial Day, 1917.

Buffalo Bill's grave is a few steps from the museum atop Lookout Mountain, with a good view of Denver and the plains. Anyone can come and see the burial place. It is marked by white pebbles. The simple legend reads: William F. Cody, 1846–1917.

The museum stands in a quiet conifer forest. First opened in 1919, it has been restored and improved over the years. A gift shop sells Indian arrowheads, Indian carpets and other fitting items.

The hours are 10 a.m.–4:30 p.m. in winter and 9 a.m.–5 p.m. in summer. Call (303) 526-0747. Small fee. For the most scenic drive, take U.S. 6 west of Denver to Golden, turn left on Nineteenth Street and proceed uphill via Lookout Mountain Road.

Lookout Mountain

Never mind, all you rock climbers! Step aside, you hardy mountaineers! Make room for some hiking tourists—the sort who can spare only a couple of hours or so for a gentle excursion into the Colorado front range. Easy mountain flower-bordered trails abound in the foothills near the state capital.

One of the least known paths curves around **Lookout Mountain,** which was first used by the Cheyenne and Arapaho Indians as a lookout. Now known as the **Beaver Brook Trail,** it is one of the state's most interesting paths, yielding views of the gorges below, dipping and climbing with a varied landscape of leaf trees and dramatic Douglas fir. Although you're close to Denver, you're quickly led away from civilization.

Instead of highways, there are fields of asters, yucca and wild roses under you. In the forests, the path is moss bordered, and spring beauties show their heads in season.

The Beaver Brook Trail makes some demands on your balance because you need to maneuver across several small boulder fields, which really amounts to an easy level of rock climbing.

17

Off The Beaten Path in ...

Start of the Beaver Brook Trail in Golden

Going on for about six miles, Beaver Brook remains blissfully quiet during the week. On Sundays, however, you sometimes see church groups and long lines of scouts and other hikers coming up from the city. If you hike up here in July and August, you'll be surrounded by lots of color. On the trail you may also spot the state flower, the blue Rocky Mountain columbine.

It's true that wildflowers bloom later at the higher elevations. By the time plants have already wilted above Golden (elevation 7,600 feet), other flowers on the Beaver Brook Trail just begin to unfold. The higher you climb, the later the growth, the smaller the flower and the colder the air.

Small Colorado plants appear and disappear with the seasons, go underground, or take many years to mature. Wonders? Certain wildflowers can sleep peacefully under the thickest snow cover, biding their time until spring. In summer, the large fields of mountain flowers on the Beaver Brook Trail Meadows give pleasure to your eyes.

The Beaver Brook Trail is within easy reach from Denver by car. Just take U.S. 6, turn left at the first traffic light (Nineteenth Street) in Golden, then drive up the curvy SR 68 for three miles. Before you get to Buffalo Bill's Grave, you spot a sign on your right: "Beaver Brook Trail," it reads. "No horses!"

Matthews-Winters Park

Surprise! Just 20 minutes west of Denver, the Big City—utter silence in a little known park. To the north, the famous Red Rocks; to the south the little hamlet of Morrison, with its antique stores.

Matthews-Winters Park derives its importance from location: the park lies astride the entrance to Mt. Vernon Canyon, which was one of the early routes to the gold fields of Central City (then known as the Gregory Diggings) and South Park. Other canyons were also used, and at each portal a town was founded to try to get a share of the quick fortune the Fifty-niners were scrambling to uncover.

The park now consists of undulating grasslands, hiking trails (also used by horses) and fields of sedges, bleached in summer, silver-green sage, purple thistles, wild roses and wild plums.

Sunflowers and chokecherries and willows lean over the gravestones and crosses of long gone pioneers: "I. R. Dean, Died August 12, 1860, aged 31 years, I am At Rest." And the marker of a younger man: "James Judy, Died September 8, 1867, Aged 21 years."

PHOTO BY JILL VIG

Hiking is a popular activity in the state

Trails run through rabbit brush and tall dill, and there's nary a sound, despite the nearby highways.

The big year here was 1859. The stagecoaches and wagons rolled through, and the new town of Mt. Vernon had a 150-horse corral. A local paper declared that "timber, stone, lime and coal are abundant in the vicinity." For a while, Mt. Vernon became a stage stop. An inn, a saloon and a schoolhouse were built, used, abandoned. Once "boasting 44 registered voters," the town of Mt. Vernon lost its place in history after the railroads arrived. And now? A few square gravestones, some crosses and wild vegetation. Not far away, next to Mt. Vernon Creek, picnic tables sit under leafy trees.

The public parking area is located off of SR 26, just south of I-70, and lies within the platted Mt. Vernon town site. The park is open from 5 a.m.–11 p.m.

Heritage Square

Have a few hours to spare? Like to browse in interesting little shops, yet get away from downtown Denver? Do your lungs crave fresh air? Solution: a 20-minute drive from the city to **Heritage Square** in Golden. Many travelers are unaware that this replica of an 1800-style village exists. Even many Denverites forget that this accumulation of Old West shops and boutiques

PHOTO BY CURTIS W. CASEWIT

Heritage Square, near Golden, is popular with tourists

is open all year. Entrance to the village is gratis. Ditto for the parking.

The 800-acre compound allows artisans to do their work. You see glassblowers, weavers, leather workers, candle makers, silversmiths, picture framers, tintype photographers, artists attending to their easels. You'll find yourself in a sweet-smelling shop of hand-dipped chocolates, study old-fashioned pewter or antiques in other establishments, talk to a hatter, admire trinkets and souvenirs of all kinds. Surprise: an Arab *Souk* (market) with Persian carpets, Lebanese tables, Saudi vases, Middle Eastern mosaic. Or enter an emporium that sells practical kitchen items like whisks, basters, wooden rolling pins, jam lid openers, Swedish potato brushes.

Heritage Square feeds your tummy as well. A western barbecue, a moderately priced restaurant, an ice cream parlor and an inexpensive *Gasthaus*, which sells bratwurst, beer and pretzels, all invite the visitor.

Nighttime attractions? The **Heritage Square Opera House**, of course. No expectations of Verdi, Puccini, Bizet, please. This theatre offers old-time melodramas, vaudeville olio, short skits, sing-alongs. The posters are seductive; a songfest may include "Bye Bye, Blackbird," "Let Me Call You Sweetheart" and "Yes, Sir! That's My Baby!" And the melodrama? The innocent should be forewarned: this melodrama invites audience participation—an "ah" for the heroine, a "booo" for the villain. The plot is as silly as the dialogue. But it all dovetails with the souvenir shops where you can buy a postcard that reads, "May all your days be bright with rainbows."

Heritage Square is busiest in summer, what with auto shows, fireworks, square dancing and many more activities. Special areas try to please children as well.

Summer hours from 10 a.m.–9 p.m.; late fall to early spring from 10 a.m.–6 p.m., Sunday from noon–6 p.m. From Denver, drive west on Sixth Avenue, or on I-70 (Exit 262) to U.S. 40 (Colfax), then one mile west. For general information, call (303) 279-2789. The address: Heritage Square, Golden, CO 80401.

Central City

The **Central City Opera House** seldom misses an opportunity to stage operas having to do with Colorado's past. During one season, for instance, the *Ballad of Baby Doe* proved to be a most appropriate work. The Baby Doe Tabor story deals with

Central City, Colorado

the lavish Colorado mining riches more than one hundred years ago.

At one point in history, Central City vied with Leadville for the bonanzas. They called Central City the Richest Square Mile on Earth. In all, some $75 million in gold was found there. Tourists can still do a bit of gold panning in nearby creeks. And through Labor Day, you can ride a recreated narrow gauge railway along the bleached mountain sides, past the old abandoned mounds of earth, mines of yesteryear.

Sloping, winding **Eureka Street** has been kept up. The red brick buildings look as well preserved as those of Denver's restored Larimer Square. Central City's pharmacy and several others stores put their oldest relics into the windows. The opera singers stay at the ancient **Teller House Hotel,** which is crammed with magnificent old clocks, armoires, rolltop desks, velvet sofas, antique phones. A rediscovery of Victorian times, still worth visiting today. (Such plushness came with an original price tag of $107,000 for the hotel.) The Teller House and the well-appointed old Opera House contrast with the miners' dwellings. They're small, modest cubes scattered across the pale gold or ochre and russet slopes.

The first frame houses sprang up during the 1860s, along with the mine dumps. Gold! Not just in a river, but in the mountain, too. A man named John Gregory had plodded to 8,500-foot-high Central City from Denver, a trip of some 35 miles with an elevation gain of over 3,000 feet.

That was in 1859. Gregory soon dug up a fortune. The word raced as fast as the spring waters of Clear Creek River. Horace Greeley, the New York editor, heard about Gregory Gulch and traveled west to take a personal look. Greeley reported: "As yet the entire population of the valley, which cannot number less than four thousand, sleep in tents or under pine boughs, cooking and eating in the open air."

A mass of prospectors swarmed into the hillsides. Some people had a grand time. A theatre was built. Sarah Bernhardt and Edwin Booth came to perform. The Teller House Hotel rose in 1872, attracting the finest artisans. Large, carved bedsteads, marble-topped commodes, tall rosewood and walnut highboys were ferried across the prairies and up the rough roads by ox team and mule, and on wood-burning trains. Central City's hotel hosted famous people. President Ulysses S. Grant, Walt Whitman, Oscar Wilde, Baron de Rothschild and assorted European noblemen and their wives all slept in Central City.

In 1874, most of the community burned down. But gold rebuilt it. Less than four years later, there was a new opera house, which still stands. Through the decades, the small, warm, intimate 750-seat theatre fetched major productions, including opera staples like *Tosca, Manon, The Merry Widow, Rigoletto* and the British D'Oyly Carte Company's *Yeoman of the Guard*.

Opening night remains Colorado's great social event. The cars climb the road along Clear Creek Canyon, the same route taken by John Gregory more than one hundred years ago.

Central City is about an hour's drive from Denver via U.S. 6. Performances take place in the Victorian Opera House, on Eureka Street, in June and July. (For exact dates and productions call (303) 571-4435.)

The Black Forest Inn

The **Black Forest Inn** at Black Hawk is worth the 15-minute detour from Idaho Springs through the picturesque Clear Creek Canyon. The restaurant is the lair of owner Bill Lorenz, a

German who built up a reputation for schnitzel, sauerbraten, goulash, pork loins, wild game and other specialties a la Deutsch. Try the oxtail soup for appetizer and order German wines or beers.

Herr Lorenz is always on hand, supervising his staff among the expected trappings of cuckoo clocks, tapestry that depict old Rhine castles, antlered trophies. The Black Forest is open all year, except for January when Herr Lorenz goes home to Germany. His inn offers meals only—no accommodations.

Hours are daily 11 a.m.–9:30 p.m.; Sundays 11 a.m.–8 p.m., closed Mondays except summer. Meals here are expensive but worth it. You reach the inn via U.S. 6 and Co. Rd. 119; turn left at Black Hawk. Phone: (303) 279-2333.

St. Mary's Glacier

They always called it a glacier. But this Colorado remnant of the Ice Age is actually an icefield, covering a steep year-round snowbowl of about ten acres. In summer, when Denver swelters in an 85-degree heat wave, it's about 45 degrees on the glacier and young people come to ski here in July and August. Other visitors to the famous snowfield bring platters or auto tubes or race downhill even on shovels. Hikers, campers and backpackers can be seen at the 11,000-foot level as they scramble uphill past the last scrub pines. A few tourists come to sit on rocks and soak up the Colorado sun.

All that eternal snow and ice make **St. Mary's Glacier** unusual, of course. The trip is a pleasant one, attracting Sunday drivers from the Big City. Once you exit I-70, you follow a creek, flanked by stands of conifers and aspen trees. After about eight miles, the road steepens and leads into a series of driver-challenging curves and serpentines. Then the valley widens and the forest thickens. You see several rushing waterfalls. At elevation 10,400 feet, you notice a free parking lot; leave your car and hike up the rocky jeep trail or follow the uphill footpaths through kinnikinnik, past the many fallen trees that slowly turn to dust. On weekends, you meet lots of families on your way up to the Glacier. People are friendly and talkative. "Been to the top yet? How was it? Do we have far to go?"

After half an hour, you see a cold lake, topped by the glacier. It's less harmless than most folks think. Mountain dwellers know St. Mary's record: each year, someone who skis too fast or careens downhill on a shovel somehow gets bruised, bloodied or even killed. On occasion, cross-country skiers are buried by an avalanche up here. In winter, the ill-prepared, ill-clothed can get frostbitten on top of the glacier, at the 11,400 foot level. The prudent know that mountains are unforgiving; these visitors only come to St. Mary's when it smiles.

Follow I-70 just past Idaho Springs; then take Exit 238, known as the Fall River Road. A 12-mile drive brings you to the parking lot and the start of your St. Mary's Glacier adventure.

Rock Climbing in the Boulder Area

It is still early when the jeep pulls into **Eldorado Springs Canyon,** swishes across an oiled road, and comes to a stop. There are four in the vehicle: three physicians and a broad-shouldered mountain climber who has roamed 20,000 foot altitudes. For a weekend, even 2,000 feet of climbing will do. As long as there is a technical challenge.

The challenge could be one of the Flatiron rocks, especially the Third. The names carry messages: Naked Edge is one of the state's hardest climbing routes; Red Garden Wall is sheer verticality.

Already, from the road, the climbers can see the dark brown slab slicing the lightening sky, daring the men. They shoulder their lead-heavy packs and wind their way to the base of the cliff. Here they unpack their gear: nylon ropes, neatly coiled, dozens of chocks—steel spikes—of all sizes and colors, water and food for an exhausting day.

At 8 a.m., the stone face still remains in the shadows. It shoots up straight. Few hand- or footholds.

The men peer up, craning their necks at the opponent. Now they fasten the hardware around their midriffs and form two parties who will attack the rock face at separate points. Here they rope in silently, purposefully. One man begins to scale his way up from the road one hundred yards to his left, then another lead starts up. In each party, only one person at a time does the climbing. Very, very slowly. When the sun finally hits the granite and the tourists arrive, the Boulder men have only gained 70 feet. For the bystander, there is not much drama here. Only precision and caution and labor. By early afternoon, the four challengers have made the top. A total gain of 800 vertical feet. The Coloradans feel a great sense of achievement.

Vertical adventures are to be found all over this state, the climbing and mountaineering magnet of Mainland U.S.A.

Colorado's average altitude is a lofty 6,800 feet; this state contains more than 75 percent of all the land above 10,000 feet in the United States. The Boulder area is especially popular.

For the good rock climber, Eldorado Springs Canyon provides many of the region's hardest challenges. Today, the magnificently sheer walls attract close to 50,000 climbing attempts each year. Hundreds of possible routes exist on the canyon's many major cliffs.

Every top cragsman or woman has a personal list of the most difficult ascents in the Boulder Mountain area, and lots of stories as well. Some of the most notorious feats are Psycho, Jules Verne, Vertigo and the Diving Board, all in Eldorado Springs or vicinity. **Boulder Canyon** and the Flatirons area feature such eloquently named hair-raisers as Death and Transfiguration, Country Club Crack and Tongo.

The Third Flatiron is one of the more famous destinations attracting many Boulder collegians. Most require two to five hours to reach the 1,400-foot crest, which happens to be even higher than New York's Empire State Building. Colorado's leading rock specialists are able to do the job in half an hour. The record is twelve minutes.

Spectators can watch the performances from below.

In essence, the sport is an elegant form of gymnastics. Strength, form and rhythm become more important than endurance. Years back, the object was to reach a wall or peak via the safest and most convenient route. After the turn of the century, small groups of Colorado mountaineers began to evolve the modern-day philosophy. Rock climbing now became an art form—a delicate vertical ballet choreographed by the peculiarities of the rock itself.

A Colorado wall can involve the mind like a chess game. The expert studies his target from level ground and then keeps studying the route all along the way up. Bill Forrest, a well-known Denver-based expert who often shows up in Eldorado Canyon, underlines this subtle interplay of mind and body. "A major part of climbing is *looking*," Forrest says. "Look with the fingers and feet as well as with the eyes. A leader must employ all senses to scrutinize a wall and to seek protection possibilities."

Top leaders choose each foot- and handhold with care. They test rock. Will it hold? Could it crumble? Is that crack too high up to be reached? Even on easier pitches experienced climbers make it a habit to pick their steps with deliberation. No hasty moves. No slipping. No falling. Besides, the climber must have three points of contact with the rock. The contact can be two hands and one foot, or one hand and two feet. (Knees are never used.) Nor do skilled cragsmen grip bushes, small trees or other vegetable holds. Plants seldom grow deep roots in rocky country.

A proper position also separates the novice from the expert. New climbers often lean *into* the mountain, hugging it. Experts know that it is better to keep the upper body *away* from the rock. So they lean out and look up. They develop rhythm. This way, they surmount every hurdle.

How do you get started? Boulder's **Colorado Mountain Club** chapter organizes a yearly school for all comers. The **Mountain Rescue Group** has taught mountaineering, and the elders of the **American Alpine Club** and the local **Sierra Club chapter** take up their members for lessons. Mountaineering schools or individual instructors are often connected with Boulder climbing equipment shops, where you can find out details. And lastly, the **University of Colorado** organizes some special summer programs for first-timers. As a result of all these and other possibilities, Boulder actually has more rock enthusiasts per capita than other cities of 72,000 inhabitants.

Actually, rock climbing isn't too difficult to learn. Any moderately athletic person can pick up basic techniques in a couple of days. ("It's the soul that counts, not the body," says one guide.) Being in condition helps.

On the Colorado cliffs, the two major maneuvers are (1) the *belay*, a stance allowing you to protect your teammates by means of a rope; and (2) the *rappel*, which helps you to get down any steep wall. Only the first step over the void takes courage; the rest of the downward journey is easy, in the company of experienced guides.

Some authorities consider **bouldering** the best practice. Bouldering is a means of training; it allows you to scale difficult rock sections close to the ground. Even experts can be seen on Eldorado Canyon boulders testing themselves against strenuous/hairy sequences of six to eight feet off the ground. This practice prepares them for similar terrain higher up.

Generally most local routes offer quick escapes if the weather turns bad. An exception: the east face of the Third Flatiron. This panoramic climb is generally underestimated by novices.

Sudden meteorological changes can be the undoing here. Other beginners may underestimate the difficulty of an ascent and overestimate their own skills. Likewise, guides warn tyros that they must never venture into the high terrain on their own. The Boulder-based Rocky Mountain Rescue Group performs an average of 120 rescue operations each year in the area. Many such missions are the result of the inexperienced getting into trouble, sometimes resulting in injuries—broken ankles, legs, backs or head traumas.

Good climbers respect these mountains and at the same time savor the aesthetics. They see the beauty of the scenery. To be sure, Eldorado Canyon seems different from one day to the next. You observe subtle light changes. The stone may now be dark blue, now orange, now golden. It can look harsh or delicate. A sudden prism of light can illuminate a meadow below and sharpen the crests above. So each trip is new. You will climb peaks in delightfully soft sunshine or under ultraviolet rays that tan even the palest faces. You drink and water never tasted so sweet. Food—any food—goes down remarkably well after the day's clambering across Colorado's rocks.

Fortunately, you're never by yourself. Solo climbing is insanity and reserved for a few rare hermits. For the average person, lone rockmanship remains nearly impossible. The climbing ropes require several people. Safety comes in numbers of two or more.

On a rope, personal values change. Speaking the truth, helping, adapting, persevering become important. Human contacts come faster. When at its best, mountaineering can bring human beings closer together. Woodrow Wilson Sayre, a climber and professor of philosophy, once put it this way in *Four Against Everest*: "Real friendship is increasingly difficult to maintain. We hurry so much, we move, we change jobs, we juggle a hundred responsibilities. How often do we see our best friend? If we hardly see them, can we really share joy and tragedy with them? I think we crave a deeper sort of friendship. If we don't have it, we miss something very important in life. Friends are made for the close warmth tested in the mountains."

Eldorado Springs is about 25 miles west of Denver via the Boulder Turnpike and SR 128; the area is 7 miles south of Boulder via SR 170.

The Magic of Mountain Botany

Mountain flowers! What a variety of life forms! Botanists estimate that there are some 6,000 species in the Rockies alone. Who can doubt it?

Just go to the Colorado foothills and then higher up, repeating your hikes each month. What a myriad of colors! Lavendar, crimson, blue brushstrokes! Bright white, butter yellow, pink! The first sign of spring brings forth a rush of Easter daisies, mountain marigolds, wild sweetpeas, fairy trumpets, pink rock hill phlox and others in many hues. Wander up in early summer to Colorado's 8,000- or 9,000-foot levels. And lo! Here, almost overnight, you'll see leafy cinquefoils, arnicas, yellow monkey flowers, and the official state flower, the blue Rocky Mountain columbine. (The latter also grows in the foothills.) In July you'll be welcomed by the star gentians, wood lilies, the mountain aster and several kinds of larkspur.

You cannot help but admire the hardiness of vegetation at the altitudes of the Rockies. How is it possible that the plants do not die under the battle conditions of winter storms? What makes tiny wildflowers get along with less oxygen and more radiation? How do some mountain flowers manage to spite the short summers and harsh climate above timberline? A sense of wonder must fill you at some mountaintop discoveries.

First of all, smallness helps. The tinier the leaves, the less resistance to the wind. In the summit meadows, known as tundra, you will discover miniature grasses, sedges and herbs. You bend down to miniflowers. If you brought a magnifying glass, you'd see details of almost-microscopic leaves. There are plants without any stems; others come with stems so short that the swirling air masses can't budge them. At the same time, the roots go deep down into the ground; a two-foot root is the two-inch plant's insurance against being ripped out by storms.

Amazing nature! Most mountain flora hold on to the day's warmth at night by closing their petals.

Mountain flowers protect themselves with tiny umbrellas or hairs, fine layers of wool, or waxy leaves that hold moisture. Mountain flowers can also adapt to the cold. In the Rockies thousands of avalanche lilies push through the snow, thus surprising the traveler with their delicate (and edible) yellow petals.

The growing season is short in Colorado. And nature has wisely arranged for most mountain flowers to be perennials so that they need not struggle each season. Such flora develop slowly but survive for several years. Other wildflowers sprout for a brief period at certain months each year. They thrive and shine under mysterious direction of sun and season, in concert with the flora elsewhere, waiting and then multiplying.

One Swiss botanist notes the wondrous cycle of those multiplying and then vanishing creations: "Storms sweep up the seeds, blow them away, and wherever they fall—sometimes in the most inauspicious places—a tiny new life tries to take root; just one little life, inconspicuous among millions and millions more. Yet this tiny plant clings, waits, grows, and—bringing forth flower, color, and fruit—to master all the adversities."

Colorado Mountain Conservation

As the vacation season grinds into high gear, park personnel gird themselves for millions of summer motorists, campers, hikers, climbers, backpackers and other visitors. Every year, travelers flock in record numbers to Colorado.

Can anything be done to lessen the impact on the fragile environment? The answer is yes.

COURTESY OF COLORADO DEPARTMENT OF PUBLIC RELATIONS

Colorado camping, either rugged or refined, is a vacation experience the entire family will long remember.

As a traveler you can do much to improve the situation in the Colorado mountains. Begin by not picking wildflowers. (In Switzerland, tourists pay a heavy fine if they're caught gathering edelweiss and some other rare species.)

Continue by not littering. Apparently one litterer creates another. Many local mountain clubs actually organize hikes for volunteer crews to pick up trash on or near hiking trails. In Estes Park the owners of the Longs Peak Inn resort periodically ride up the trails on pack horses with saddle bags to pick up empty cigarette packages and candy wrappers. At the nearby YMCA, mountain guides pick up the empty beer cans of the careless Sunday masses. The head of a Colorado environment group says: "Some tourists are poor stewards of the Beautiful Country. They drive spikes into trees, use privies for target practice, shatter the forest stillness with radio or TV set. They leave initials in red paint on the rockface."

Please, refrain from cutting your initials into trees, a rather common and brutal practice.

If you happen to visit a Western ghost town this summer, take nothing but photographs. Forget about carrying off a souvenir piece of an abandoned cabin. Future visitors will be grateful to view the complete ghost town.

The environment credo should also interest people who toss bottle caps into resort streams. Please don't. The cap may get stuck in a fish's throat.

Lastly, one local conservationist suggests that the state adopt a slogan that warns, "There is only *one* Colorado. Tread gently. Make it last!"

Colorado's Western Mountains Via I-70

Victorian Georgetown

In autumn, the wind whistles through the well-kept streets of **Georgetown**, rattling the windows of the impeccable Victorian houses. The winter snows pile up high here, and spring is slow to come at elevation 8,500 feet above sea level. The mountains rise so steeply on all four sides of Georgetown that even the summers are cool; the sun shines for only a few hours.

Yet this community 45 miles west of Denver has more ambiance, more sightseeing, more genuine concern for its own history than most Colorado cities. It is special in its own way. The city fathers have spent six-figure sums to rebuild and preserve the pink brick houses, the old-time saloons, the museums that conjure up the last century of gold and silver riches. The antique shops, silversmiths and weavers are among the best in the state. The craft shops are different, real, worth browsing in, and much better than those of Vail or other fancy ski resorts to the west.

Unlike Vail, which rose from a cow pasture, Georgetown is a historic community.

On a clear spring day in 1859 two prospecting brothers, George and David Griffith, struggled their way up Clear Creek searching for minerals. Unsuccessful at the other mining camps in Colorado, they reached out for new untried land, and this time they had luck—they found gold.

After the discovery, the Griffith brothers did a highly unusual thing for prospectors—instead of just digging up the mountain and leaving with their wealth, they brought their entire family out from Kentucky to live permanently in their valley. The tiny settlement they founded became known as George's Town, and although no more significant strikes were made, it grew steadily for five years.

Then, in 1884, assays showed an extremely high silver content. The boom was on. Over the next 30 years, the mines in and around Georgetown produced over $200 million worth of silver. The town became known as the Silver Queen of the Mountains—and in 1868, it was named Georgetown.

By 1880, 10,000 people made the city their home. The building of fortunes, houses and reputations flourished. Elaborate mansions attested to wealth. Hotels served the finest cuisine in gilt

33

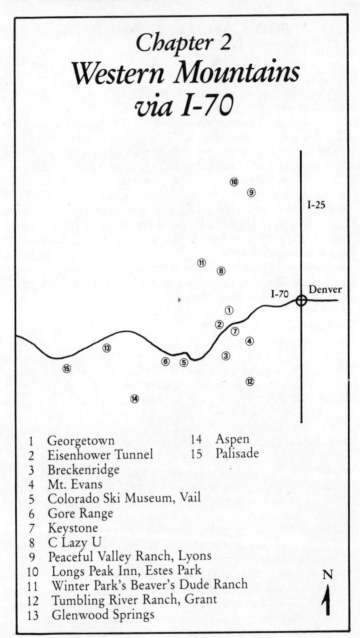

Chapter 2
Western Mountains
via I-70

1 Georgetown
2 Eisenhower Tunnel
3 Breckenridge
4 Mt. Evans
5 Colorado Ski Museum, Vail
6 Gore Range
7 Keystone
8 C Lazy U
9 Peaceful Valley Ranch, Lyons
10 Longs Peak Inn, Estes Park
11 Winter Park's Beaver's Dude Ranch
12 Tumbling River Ranch, Grant
13 Glenwood Springs
14 Aspen
15 Palisade

rooms with elegant furniture. An Opera House brought Broadway productions and favorite classical operas to the wealthy.

All this came to an abrupt end; the silver panic of 1893 hit hard, with silver prices dropping to almost nothing. Mines, mills and livelihoods vanished. The town became the ghost of its past glory.

Georgetown rested for over six decades. Then tourism came, and interstate highways transported millions of tourists to the high mountains.

Unlike other Colorado mining towns, Georgetown was never totally destroyed by fire, so today it has more that 200 carefully preserved historic buildings.

Luckily, too, Georgetown passed a historic preservation ordinance many years ago. The local historical society is serious about its purpose. One of Georgetown's landmarks is the French-style **Hotel de Paris**, now a museum full of Tiffany fixtures, lace curtains, hand-carved furniture. (Open June to September only, 9 a.m.–5 p.m. Small charge.) Georgetown has several Victorian mansions worth seeing. During the first two December weekends, a well-known Christmas market with small booths and outdoor stalls beckons.

For more information, write the Chamber of Commerce, P.O. Box 667, Georgetown, CO 80444-0667. From Denver, Georgetown can be reached via I-70 west in about an hour.

This old mining town is attractive the year round, especially in fall

Colorado's Eisenhower Tunnel

"Nearly impossible!" a geologist said when a Colorado financier first suggested a long tunnel through the Continental Divide during the thirties. "Unpredictable rock!" other geologists warned in 1941. The drilling of a pilot bore already gave a clue to the unstable rock strata of the area in the Colorado Rockies. Steel linings buckled in the exploratory shaft. For three decades, tunnel builders battled the mountain some 58 miles west of Denver. Lack of money, politics, explosions, fires and, most of all, geological problems all thwarted the builders. A tunnel engineer later summed it up better than anyone. "We were going by the book," he said. "But the damned mountain couldn't read!"

Fortunately, the 8,941-foot-long **Eisenhower Tunnel** was eventually drilled despite the obstacles. The tunnel pierces the Colorado Rockies and saves the motorist ten miles over the twisting and turning highway that crosses Loveland Pass. Since the tunnel opened in 1973, drivers need no longer expose themselves to fierce storms and howling winds of the pass. No more jackknifed trucks, stranded cars, vehicles swept off the highway ledges by avalanches, rock slides or icy curves taken too fast. One of North America's best known mountain passes was finally tamed.

Its story is fascinating. For a hundred years, since the days when railroads were first reaching across the continent, men have worked and dreamed of tunneling through the Continental Divide here, where it's narrowest.

Everyone agreed that the existing roads across the 12,000-foot-high mountain crests presented some perils and inconveniences. In the twenties and thirties, a motor trip was still considered a major undertaking on the 12-foot wide Loveland Pass road. The local papers claimed that such travel resembled a stunt, and called the motorists undaunted. One eyewitness reported that, "Mud and a steep grade combine to balk all but the highest built cars." In summer, automobiles sometimes plummeted from the steep road, and hikers could see old hulks rusting in the valleys. The worst times were in winter when Colorado's east and west slopes became cut off from one another. Eventually, irate citizens put placards on their auto bumpers that read, "We demand a Tunnel!"

It became clear that only a tunnel would make travel possible at all seasons, besides reducing distances across the Rockies. In

January, 1937, a mountain community leader proposed a ten-mile tunnel. It took four years until the Colorado Highway Department began to drill a 5,483-foot pioneer bore. World War II brought the work to a halt, despite much clamor in the mountain towns and in the Colorado state capital. One November day in 1947, a large group of marchers showed up at the statehouse in Denver, calling for action. At the same time, signs appeared in front range cafes and restaurants that demanded a Loveland Pass Tunnel Now!

Before long, the tunnel idea moved into high gear. The project was advertised and bids were to be opened. Unfortunately, only one bid was received, which brought the tunnel idea to another standstill.

In short, the mountain giant had won. No one wanted to take it on. In the pilot bore, the ceilings gradually caved in, and inspectors reported gushing water and musty odors. Engineers told the press that men would have to work and live under impossible climatic conditions at an 11,000-foot altitude, and that it would be extremely difficult to transport materials to the site. Attention-seeking politicians showed up in the tunnel bore, garbed in yellow slickers, rubber boots and impressive miner's hats. The test shaft's air quickly ended the visit.

During the early 1960s, the tunnel reared its rocky head again; it found its way into the Congressional Record. "In a few years a tunnel will be carved through solid granite. It will be an engineering marvel."

Work progressed only slowly. The Continental Divide would not bow to the nine firms that had been welded into one contractor. Sometimes, as many as 1,100 men sweated and coughed in three shifts inside the mountain. Mounted on three-tiered drilling platforms, a dozen giant drills poked into the tunnel's brain. The attack of these massive drilling machines were followed by blasts of water to wash out the fresh holes. The racket was tremendous, and bearded hard-hatted miners wore thick plastic ear muffs lined with sponge rubber.

After just three months of penetration, workmen noticed that a large area had shifted, buckling some steel linings. Total costs soon soared above the original bids of $49 million to $100 million, with the tunnel still acting up. On Feb. 13, 1969, miners had to run for safety as some walls 600 feet inside the west portal started to disintegrate. Dismay was equally great when the granite resisted altogether. The contractor requested permission to attack one fault zone with a specially designed shield. The five-story, twelve-drill, 22-foot monster weighed 670 tons with its tailpiece. The machine was capable of exerting a push of 20 million pounds.

The shield was first housed in a mammoth chamber near the west portal. Came the historic day when the engineering wonder began its journey into the tunnel. The Highway Department's fanfare—and the newspapers' excitement—proved to be somewhat premature: the shield advanced only 70 feet in less than a month. On Sept. 4, 1969, the device ground to a sudden standstill; its 34 roller bearings were stuck. The shield's mentors redesigned it to move on skids. This time, alas, the machine budged just seven inches. The earth pressures were too much, and the expensive colossus had to be abandoned in the tunnel, where it still lies today, cemented into the walls.

No further progress was made for more than a year after this million-dollar failure. The tunnel designers brought in qualified consultants at stiff fees from all over the United States. To no avail. Finished sections still threatened to fall apart. On occasion, the whole mass of granite, gneiss and schist seemed to be moving. In some areas, the rock resembled clay, and dust kept squeezing through every crevice. In the collapsing areas, some rock could be "nailed" to a more stable surface; in other sections, curved supports helped distribute the pressures. Sometimes, the only solution was to double the support beams. All these unforeseen emergencies and the additional materials consumed a fortune in man-hours.

There were other problems. About 60 miners walked out when a woman was hired as an engineer. Twice, the workmen walked out to protest poor ventilation.

One December day, a fire brought work to a complete stop. No one knows for sure how the flames started some 4,000 feet inside the western tunnel section. An acetylene torch—and some straw—may have touched off the fire. To smother it, the outside air supply had to be shut off and the smoke assaulted the men's lungs. Would gas pockets cause an explosion? The possibility seemed real enough. Almost a week passed before work could continue.

Barely three months later, a $200,000 explosion rocked the concrete operation at the west entrance. This time, there may have been an equipment malfunction. The mishap destroyed the huge boiler, the concrete-mixing machinery, 5,000 gallons of oil, a large propane tank and the company ambulance.

The job had been enormous on all levels: The excavation alone had taken 524,000 cubic yards out of a mountain bent on creating mischief and causing deaths. The tunnel actually took five lives—three in accidents, two from heart attacks at the high elevation. There were more than 50 broken arms, legs and ankles. No one could count the hours of anguish felt by the contractors, engineers and workmen about whether the job would ever get finished. The mountain giant constantly held out its fist for more money. The original Highway Department estimate—made in 1937—was $1 million dollars. The cost exceeded $115 million for one bore.

Yet all this effort and expenditure represented a mere start because the tunnel could at first accommodate only one lane of traffic each way. The Interstate Highway system must be four lanes, so a second section was dug by some 500 workers at a cost of another $225 million. The now complete Eisenhower Tunnel opened for traffic on Dec. 21, 1979. Lots of bad rock gave the engineers and drilling crews plenty of trouble.

But the job was at last accomplished. "The damned mountain finally knew the score," said one engineer. "Like it or not, we *did* get through!"

The Eisenhower Tunnel is 58 miles west of Denver via I-70.

Historic Breckenridge

Breckenridge is the perfect little Colorado frontier town— one of the few that was rebuilt and is now well preserved and thriving.

When a group of European journalists visited many of the state's resorts, Breckenridge seemed to delight them more than most others. Why? Here were all the earmarks of the Old Gold Rush West: the little Victorian houses with their columns and crenelations, the clapboard structures of the miners, beautifully repainted, and store windows filled with antiques. Midwesterners and easterners feel the same way; they get the chance to let children relive United States history.

The ski slopes are still named for the old mines in the area—Gold King, Wellington, Bonanza, Cashier, Sizzler, Silverthorne—these were the names that excited the gold hunters more than a century ago.

Breckenridge is actually one of Colorado's oldest towns. In August, 1859 the first gold-seekers came streaming across the

Divide Pass to pan gold in the waters of the Blue River. Later, a silver lode started a second boom.

By 1861 some 5,000 people lived in and near Breckenridge. Summit County then extended as far as the Utah line and was one of 17 counties comprising Colorado Territory. It has since been whittled down to 615 square miles. Then, as now, Breckenridge was the county seat.

More than $30 million in gold was taken out of the district during its heyday. Most of that was from placer and lode mining. Later on, gold dredges came to tear up the countryside, leaving the great piles of rocks still to be seen along the Blue and Swan rivers, as well as along French Creek. Dredging came to a halt about 1938.

In the early 1960s, Breckenridge became a year-round resort, at the same time maintaining its century-old status as a former mining community.

Development moved ahead when the ski area opened in the early sixties. The runs were at first short but fairly varied, and always aimed at families who could meet for lunch at the handsome Alpine base lodge. Soon, the town attracted a number of good people who built second homes in the serene forests.

Breckenridge is a good choice for the family in search of a winter vacation without pretense: snowmobiling, ice fishing, easy skiing on the simply laid out ski runs, tobogganing, snowshoeing, bowling, sightseeing. Rates here are expensive, but most ski resorts are in this state.

To amuse the tourists, a yearly Pack Burro race takes place at the end of July from Fairplay through Breckenridge to Mosquito Pass. In this world championship race, contestants run alongside their loaded burros for about four hours, going 26 miles up hill and dale. Entry rules? "No needles, electric prods, narcotics, clubs or whips. No firearms. No riding of burros, but running alongside instead."

Breckenridge is 88 miles west of Denver via I-70. For more information: P.O. Box 1058, Breckenridge, CO 80424; (303) 453-2368.

Mt. Evans Highway

"It was awesome," former Miami resident Steve Cohen told friends in Florida. "We looked down at the passing clouds. You felt as though you'd reached the top of the world."

The traveler was referring to the highest paved auto road in the United States, leading from Idaho Springs, west of Denver, to the top of 14,264-foot-high **Mt. Evans.** The mountain first attracted gold-hungry prospectors during the nineteenth century; it was named in 1870 after Gov. John Evans. A few years earlier, famous artist Albert Bierstadt and a friend had climbed it. Bierstadt's paintings express the grandeur of this and other high Colorado peaks.

Pick a sunny summer day to make your drive up to the summit. Unlike on Pikes Peak, in Colorado Springs, you need to pay no toll to reach the top of Mt. Evans. Keep in mind that the road above the 10,600 foot level is only open from late June through Labor Day; if you want to conquer the peak in winter, you'll have to do so on snowshoes or cross-country skis.

What are the attractions of this summer drive? For one thing, you get to see a lot of scenery. The motorist has a choice of two approaches to the mountain—you can arrive from Denver via Bergen Park and return via Idaho Springs or vice versa. En route to the base of Mt. Evans, you'll pass large fertile meadows, dense lodge pole forests, aspen trees, ponderosa pine, Douglas fir, thick bushes of wild raspberries; you can see chipmunks and squirrels.

You may want to stop at placid **Echo Lake**, where you notice families angling for trout, picnickers enjoying their lunch, or hikers setting out for the trails that captivated painter Bierstadt so many years ago.

After Thanksgiving, the lake freezes over completely. You can skate across it on your narrow cross-country skis and reach numerous trails that yield great views. Even in summer, it gets cool up here, so dress warmly for the occasion. Indeed, scientists have established the theory that as you climb a thousand feet in the Rockies, your upward journey can be compared to a 200-mile journey north, with the cooler air in each zone on the way up—and in each vegetation belt—to match. Spring, therefore, comes a little late. Above Echo Lake, you wander through the tundra; you can study the small grasses, sedges, herbs and the almost microscopic plants with miniflowers.

To be sure, the Mt. Evans drive can be an educational one, especially for children. If you take a close look at the ancient bristlecone pines, for instance, you will quickly understand that these and other trees must fight a fierce survival battle at these high altitudes.

Every dwarfed bristlecone or leaning Douglas fir up here

tells a story of blizzards and summer storms, of blazing sunlight followed by rains. The weather destroys any exposed buds and conifer seeds, limiting their reproduction. Some trees are bent and twisted from the wind. The sun at these elevations bleaches trees; the lightning blackens and splits some of them. At timberline, the little array of trees becomes sparse; now only single isolated soldiers face the sky's hail cannons.

Above timberline, in Colorado's Alpine Life Zone, you spy different animals, too. Marmot often show up, and ptarmigan birds; some people have even reported bighorn sheep and mountain goats. ("Don't feed them," advises the U.S. Forest Service. "They sometimes bite.")

The upper reaches of Mt. Evans are also dotted with lakes: At 11,700 feet you'll spot Lincoln Lake; it's 800 feet below the highway. Then at 12,830 feet, Summit Lake awaits, complete with a short trail to overlook the picturesque Chicago Lakes, some 1,400 feet below. (The Forest Service warns parents not to let their kids run around too much because of the sudden dropoffs. The highway has no guard rails.)

Finally, you can make your motorized conquest of the summit, at 14,264 feet, where the clouds may actually be below you, as they often are on airline flights. The final few feet are by trail. Catch your breath: The air is thinner than in the plains, of course; so it's wise to walk slowly and not to overexert yourself on the summit. You'll see a lot of Colorado from the top of Mt. Evans, and your children will talk about the sights for a long time afterward.

You can start your tour on I-70. Use Exit 240 in Idaho Springs, then follow SR 103 along Clear Creek to Echo Lake and SR 5 to the Mt. Evans summit. For additional scenery and a change of pace, return to Denver via Squaw Pass Road and Bergen Park. The distances are moderate: it's just 28 miles from Idaho Springs, for example, to the summit of Mt. Evans.

Colorado Ski Museum

A ski museum? Yes, Colorado's only one and one of the few such historical gathering places in the United States. Founded in 1976, the **Colorado Ski Museum** reaches back to the old miners of the last century who raced in the Rockies surrounding their camps, competing against one another on long wooden boards, holding a long staff in one fist for braking. The museum contains a magnificent, enlarged 1859 etching of Snowshoe

Thompson, the Norwegian who skied from camp to camp in severe blizzards. He delivered the mails, candy and medicines to the marooned miners.

Here are the photos and artifacts of skiing clergymen like Father John Lewis Dyer, who brought the gospel to Colorado's historic gold towns, and the stories of sheepherders and trappers who braved the snows in the nineteenth century on nine-foot enormous wooden contraptions with crude leather straps holding their boots. (Some of the men used baling wire to keep the ski shovel curved during summer storage.) Mementoes of the first long-ago jumpers will fascinate the viewers; photos show them taking off from knolls or flying through the air, equipment sometimes falling off meters above ground.

Do you want to learn more about the first ski lifts? The Colorado Ski Museum actually displays the drive mechanism, pictures of the first rope tows and photos of funny "grippers," which latched on to the moving ropes. The localized history of chairlifts, gondolas (including a gondola rescue), ski patrol toboggans, the first U.S. Army Snow Tanks and the first ski area snow packing and grading gear can all be seen here. Any student of ski equipment can learn much about the development of skis, bindings, boots, poles, even the first ski suits, knicker-bockers, parkas, or the women's fashions of still earlier days: ladies skied in black skirts to the ankles.

The history of Colorado's famous Tenth Mountain Division is well illustrated; indeed, an entire room is devoted to the Mountain Troopers and their initial camps and wartime exploits. If the viewer is curious about methods of avalanche fighting, or up-to-date ski racing or the history of plush, urban, expensive Vail, it's all here in the very center of Vail, next door to the sleek Bank, a few steps from the five-star Lodge at Vail and near the ski slopes themselves. In the museum, a second story even offers a little theatre for gratis ski movies. And plaques contain the pictures and biographies of Colorado Ski Hall of Fame members—a somewhat politicized assembly of engineers and entrepreneurs, ski makers and ski teachers.

The museum is free to all comers; donations accepted. Open daily from noon–5 p.m. except Mondays; closed during the slow May and October seasons. Colorado Ski Museum, P.O. Box 1976, Vail, CO 81658; (303) 476-1876.

The British on the Gore Range

Two hours west of Denver, in some of the state's most impressive mountains, is the **Gore Range**. In Vail itself, you'll see the Gore Creek, especially in summer. Gore Mountain, Gore Wilderness—who in the world was Gore?

You might call him one of the most interesting visitors who ever roamed through Colorado.

The best way to get acquainted with him might be on Gore Pass. Here, a bronze plaque is visible beside the highway, at elevation 9,000 feet.

The words on the bronze may pique your curiosity: "Here in 1854 crossed Sir St. George Gore, an Irish Baronet bent on slaughter of game and guided by Jim Bridger. For three years he scoured Colorado, Montana and Wyoming accompanied usually by forty men, many carts, wagons, hounds ad unexampled camp luxuries."

Lord Gore's party, we learn, dispatched "more than 2000 buffalo, 1600 elk and deer, and 100 bears," among others.

Lord Gore marched here with his large retinue of porters

Hunting was nothing new in a land where European trappers and fur traders had already searched all of Colorado for beaver. But Lord Gore set a record; besides, no one matched his style. The Baronet had brought most of his retinue of hunters and even some porters from Ireland; his safari caravan eventually accumulated 112 horses, 21 carts, 30 wagons and four dozen hunting dogs. Sir George roamed the mountains for many months, shooting grizzly bear, antelope and other animals and making elegant camp at night, complete with silver service and rare wines.

His Lordship could afford the "unexampled camp luxuries." For one thing, his income exceeded $200,000, which was quite a sum during the mid-1850s. For another, the Irish nobleman had a taste for gourmet cuisine and rare wines—and the cooks and servants to attend to his needs. His hunting guide was frontier hero Jim Bridger, no less. Lord Gore had gone to school in Oxford, and his aristocratic tastes included various mansions in Ireland and houses in East Sussex.

Lord Gore's hunt is still spoken of by school children in the area. And thanks to the Historical Society of Colorado, future visitors to the region will be reminded of the Irishman and his exploits through the bronze plaque.

The summit of Gore Pass and the plaque are 17 miles west of Kremmling and can be reached from Denver via U.S. 40. The Forest Service has provided picnic grounds on the pass. Vail can be reached by driving south on SR 9, then U.S. 6 west.

Keystone Lodge

Just where is Colorado's best mountain hotel? If you speak of intimacy, class, decor and people who work there, the **Keystone Lodge** qualifies on all counts. It is among this biased writer's favorites. Begin with location—just 75 miles west of Denver, on the west side of the gleaming Loveland Pass.

The low-slung Keystone Lodge (a deluxe accommodation) has only 152 rooms and the exterior can fool you—grey and functional like the hotels in the French Alps. But step inside and you're swept up by the rightness of the decor; handwoven multicolored tapestry, bright carpets, rainbow curtains. And the rooms? No cost was spared: imported German chrome door handles, English carpets, thick velour towels, flawless cabinetry, deft use of wood and glass—themes that also continue in Keystone's many deluxe condominiums.

Off The Beaten Path in ...

Keystone, Colorado — Planters full of wildflowers from the nearby mountains adorn Keystone Village, where summertime visitors enjoy shopping, dining and nightlife, plus sailing and kayaking on Keystone Lake.

Everything seems one notch better at this resort: the spacious jacuzzis, the spectacular indoor-outdoor pool, year-round tennis facilities, speed and figure skating and a wide choice of restaurants (try the Garden Room *a deux*, with French tableside service). Consider the snap and class of the Keystone Lodge staff: polite bellboys in dark-blue blazers *and* ties greet you under the hotel's porte cochère, front desk clerks almost stand at attention, trained maids turn down the bed at night, skilled, professional waiters—ah, a last bastion where one strives for excellence!

The lodge is especially charming in summer when the adjacent lake is full of boaters and surrounded by a flower-lined footpath and lovely cafes with umbrellas. (In winter, the lake is used by skaters.)

Unlike the skyscraper cities encountered at some Colorado resorts, Keystone's designers managed to let the surrounding condos, townhouses and homes-for-rent blend into the forested landscape. The complexes are named for the outdoors, such as Columbine, Honeysuckle, Goldenrod, Blue Grouse, or Bristlecone. Moreover, condo accommodations reach across 2,000 acres, with free shuttle bus connections to all the amenities. Somehow, during the most severe snowstorms, the crews manage to plow the parking lots. The condo apartments are fully furnished, including dishes, silver, pots and pans, even extra pillows and blankets. The tariff here always depends on size and ranges from expensive to deluxe.

Each complex has its own swimming pools, whirlpools and saunas. And all quarters are served by a 24-hour switchboard.

Among the resort's restaurants, the **Garden Room** (deluxe) is recommended for its impeccable service and authentic French food. If you can afford it, try the cozy-smooth year-round **Keystone Ranch** (deluxe) on the golf course; this old homestead is agreeably quiet and aristocratic-western, and complete with dining by the fireplace. The **Navigator** (expensive) is a seafood house by the lake; Keystone's **Brasserie** (inexpensive) has a good Italian menu.

Once at the Keystone Lodge, even hard-to-please ski writers will be swayed by the civility, luxury and efficiency that make this first-class hotel a rare find.

The Keystone Lodge (Box 38, Keystone, CO 80435; (303) 468-4242) is 75 miles west of Denver via I-70 and U.S. 6.

Colorado Dude Ranches

The horse trip leads to a sunny meadow full of wildflowers. A few ghost houses, with caved-in roofs and sagging walls, the wood evenly bleached by the sun. Later, the party rides on. There is an excited breathlessness about the journey across two brooks, through thickets of willows and other bushes, then slowly down a steep, rocky slope. Caution and a touch of the primitive. The riders are in tune with the mountain and alone with their thoughts. It is quiet except for the slight creak of the leather saddles and the clicking of the hoofs.

The vacationers are far away from the highrises and super highways. The riders arrive for breakfast at a sunny forest clearing. Everyone sits down on long logs. The coffee steams. The cowboys fry eggs for all. The mountains say good morning.

A dude ranch vacation! What an unusual concept!

Ask other travelers to share their experiences with you. They'll speak about the informality, the privacy, the utter friendliness of Colorado's guest ranches. What with an average of 15 to about 100 guests, the mood is calm, relaxed, and the owners really care about you. Families, couples, newlyweds are pampered. If you arrive with a large party, you can write ahead for spacious quarters. At some hostelries, you can also rent cabins.

Colorado's dude ranches often have children's programs as well.

The names say much: C Lazy U Ranch. Tumbling River. Peaceful Valley Dude Ranch. Endearing places in romantic isolated Colorado locations. Some of them still breed cattle or horses.

A Colorado dude ranch vacation is one of the most self-satisfying genuine holidays available today. The air is clean, days are warm, evenings cool, and the mountain scenery absolutely spectacular.

At first primitive, the accommodations now range from rustic to deluxe ratings such as Five Star by Mobile travel guides and Exceptional by AAA (American Automobile Association).

Colorado boasts well over 50 dude ranches, generally located in the scenic mountain regions. Activities are varied and informal. Life on the ranch resort is geared for the ultimate in easy relaxation. Guests are encouraged to set their own pace.

The essence of these cowboy-style vacations becomes clear when you read the greeting on a wall of one typical guest ranch on the Wyoming-Colorado border:

Guest, you are welcome here;

Do as you please.
Go to bed when you want to
And get up at your ease.
You don't have to thank us
Or laugh at our jokes.
Say what you like,
You're one of the folks.

You may ride all day every day or merely lounge by the heated pool and take in the pure mountain air. You don't even have to swim if you don't want to. Trail rides can be a few hours to half a day or full day with a picnic. Steak fry rides are popular, too. At night, the dudes head down a pine-scented trail in the moonlight; you gaze up at the Milky Way.

A Colorado dude ranch is a small, self-contained world where you ride away from city life as well. There are lots of horse trails for novices, guided breakfast rides, ghost town rides, and even six-day rides into the wilderness. Some dude ranches arrange river rafting trips or you can rent a jeep. Archery, boating, golf are common. Chaises abound.

The phenomenon is uniquely western and especially enjoyable in the Colorado mountains where summers are never too hot or too cold. You're therefore outdoors much of the time. While adults rest or play, children have their own supervised

PHOTO BY JOHN FISCHER

This is one of Colorado's most luxurious dude ranches

49

programs. Much of the clientele returns every year. Most stay at least a week to ten days.

How much does a dude ranch vacation cost? Much less than you'd expect. If you settle on an average western place, you can have an unforgettable week for half or a third of what an ocean cruise would cost. Everything is included. Such vacations mean honest value; the customers can always rely on meals that are well cooked and served family-style, which allows you to get acquainted with other guests. At one ranch, about a two-hour drive from Denver, the breakfasts and dinners consist of huge eat-all-you-want buffets. In the morning, you'll *want* to ride off some of those calories—and get a good tan in the process.

Consider these suggestions for a dude ranch holiday. Colorado's famous **C Lazy U Ranch** features tennis courts, skeet ranges, cruise-ship style shuffleboard, and even a golf course. Naturally, there is an outdoor pool. A cocktail bar and the elegant dining appeal to many guests here. Organization is superb. Rates are deluxe. In winter Granby's C Lazy U becomes a cross-country ski center. The ranch is closed in April and May.

PHOTO BY CURTIS W. CASEWIT

The owners of the Peaceful Valley Dude Ranch built this Austrian church; it is used for weddings.

Take I-70 west of Denver to Idaho Springs. Seven miles west of Idaho Springs, turn right on U.S. 40 (Exit 232 at Empire Junction) to Granby. Three miles west of Granby, turn right on SR 125. After 3-1/2 miles, turn right at the C Lazy U gate. For more information: C Lazy U Ranch, P.O. Box 378B, Granby, CO 80446; (303) 887-3344.

At the large 150-guest **Peaceful Valley Ranch** in Lyons, Colorado, you find a main lodge and many chalets, plus the giant stables. Much of the heating comes from solar panels. And, unexpectedly, the owners built an Austrian-style, onion-steepled church for guests. (Karl and Mabel Boehm encourage churchgoing on Sunday morning and they invite a pastor for the service.)

The Peaceful Valley Ranch is best known for its summer square dancing activities; the Boehms employ a caller. This establishment has its own tennis court, a special teenage program, scout trips to ghost towns and even English riding instruction. The rates are moderate here. Lyons is easy to reach from Denver via the Boulder Turnpike, then continue via SR 7 and SR 72. For more information: Star Route, Lyons, CO 80540; (303) 747-2582.

The **Longs Peak Inn and Guest Ranch**, nine miles south of Estes Park, enjoys one of the most spectacular locations, directly under 14,000-foot-high Longs Peak. Accommodations are available in charming chalets and at the main lodge, which also serves excellent meals. (The owners are professional restaurateurs.) A horse stable, small bar, an outdoor pool, lots of Ping-Pong and stocked fishing ponds are among the many other attractions. From Estes Park, which is often mentioned in this book, take SR 7 to the ranch. American Plan rates include all meals. (Expensive, but one of the best values in the state.) For more information: Bob or Virginia Akins, Longs Peak Inn and Guest Ranch, Longs Peak Route, Estes Park, CO 80517; (303) 586-2110.

Or consider Winter Park's **Beaver's Dude Ranch**, a close 67 miles from Denver. The place has welcomed vacationers for some 40 years now. Many changes took place through the decades. The main lodge with its red gothic towers is still there. But you'll also find a new *gemuetlich* living room where you can drink a beer or a hot toddy at night.

In winter, the complex has its own sleigh for family rides,

PHOTO BY H. WILLIAM DENSHAM

Some Colorado dude ranches have swimming pools!

its private 20 miles of quiet cross-country ski trails and jacuzzis for weary downhill schussers.

Beaver's became a "village" some years ago when the owner added 165 contemporary condominiums that sit among the conifers. The units come with native stone fireplaces and mellow wood walls; skylights bring in the sun. Everything here—the large sofas, the heavy armchairs and the carpets—reflect earth colors. Room rates at the lodge are moderately priced but the elegant condos are expensive. You reach Winter Park via U.S. 40. For more information: Beaver's Dude Ranch, P.O. Box 43G, Winter Park, CO 80482; (303) 726-5212.

The **Tumbling River Ranch** in Grant seems hewn out of native rock and local wood. At night, you can hear the tumbling river under your window. The ranch stands at 9,200 feet above sea level, and, overhead, the stars stand out clearly. The ranch not only features horse activities but a handsome outdoor pool sheltered by glass panes. The food is excellent and you get lots of personal attention from the owners, the Gordons.

Grant is a short trip southwest from Denver via U.S. 285. For more information: Tumbling River Ranch, Grant, CO 80448; (303) 838-5981.

And make a note of the **Colorado Dude and Guest Ranch Association** for more ranches: Box 300, Tabernash, CO 80478.

Glenwood Springs

What is one of the most unforgettable sights and experiences in this tourist-happy state? It's **Glenwood's 600-foot-long hot springs** with happy heads of visitors bobbing in the steam, adults doing their hydrotherapy, small children riding rubber ducks, and—lo!—high mountains on all sides. Surrounded by the Rockies, with views of conifers and meadows, these thermal waters *are* relaxing. The Ute Indians discovered them and already spoke of "miraculous healing powers." The Aspen, Colorado, mining kings used those hot springs for relaxation. A famed architect, imported from Vienna, Austria, built the bathhouses here in 1890, and soon assorted American presidents came to visit Glenwood's mineral spa and "Natatorium."

Today, the recreational, swimming—and walking—part is kept at 85 to 95 degrees (29–32 degrees Celsius); hotter outdoor waters (100–104 degrees, 38–40C) are also available, fed by more than 3-1/2 million gallons. Swimmers relish the almost unlimited space in the pool while former hospital patients or the

One of the largest warm-water hot springs pools in the world, the Glenwood Hot Springs Pool delights both summer and winter visitors.

temporarily lame—like skiers recuperating from broken legs—enjoy the medical benefits. To be sure, scientists point out that the hot springs contain cornucopia elements including magnesium, calcium, sulphates, bicarbonates, phosphates and silica.

Some travelers recline much of the day in deck chairs around the two-block-long pool—Colorado's version of the *dolce vita*. No Roman bath could match Glenwood's pure air and mountain views, however. For extra luxury, the nearby **vapor baths** feature massages, plus natural saunas.

Glenwood Springs may be one of the state's most interesting communities—historically, economically, scenically—yet it never got the kind of attention accorded to Aspen (41 miles to the southeast), or overcrowded, overbuilt Vail (59 miles) or Denver, some 158 miles to the east. Buses, rental cars—and even Amtrak trains—connect travelers daily from the Colorado state capital with Glenwood. To reach it from Denver, you use busy I-70 through Glenwood Canyon, which, steep rock walls, Colorado River and all, reminds you of a narrow Grand Canyon. Unfortunately, and controversially, a segment of the interstate has been widened; man intruded on mountains.

Glenwood Springs is the gateway to some of Colorado's most dramatic and most photographed peaks, like the Maroon Bells near Snowmass, or lone, spectacular Mt. Sopris, which you notice from almost everywhere in the region. The immense **White River National Forest** offers backpackers much wilderness. Fishermen rave about the catches of trout (rainbows or browns) in the surrounding rivers—the Roaring Fork, the Frying Pan and the Colorado. Glenwood has guides that take you rafting and kayaking. And hiking possibilities are plentiful. (Head for the Hanging Lake trail complete with waterfall; it's one of the local favorites.) Hunters come to the region for elk, deer, grouse, waterfowl.

Both town and area are blessed with accommodations for every pocketbook. Economy travelers welcome the numerous campgrounds, or inexpensive little cabins flanking the soothing rivers. Large and small motels abound. The historic **Hotel Colorado** (see next entry) is open all year.

You're never far from the parades with floats, carnivals and other festivities of Glenwood's **Strawberry Days**, yearly fishing contests, various rodeos, the **Fall Art Festival**, and the quiet mountain paths under a blue sky.

And to be sure, your hotel or inn will never be far from

Noted for superb whitewater conditions, the Colorado and Roaring Fork Rivers offer guided rafting, kayaking and float fishing trips throughout the summer season.

Glenwood Springs's famous year-round outdoor pool—a thermal wonder that doesn't force you to *swim*; you can just walk through most of it, for your health's sake.

It all adds up to quite a vacation destination.

Chamber of Commerce, 1102 Grand Avenue, Glenwood Springs, CO 81601; (303) 945-6589. The community is easy to reach from Denver by rental car, bus or train. Motorists use I-70. The distance to Denver is 158 miles.

Hotel Colorado

While in Glenwood Springs, don't fail to take a leisurely stroll through the stately **Hotel Colorado**, which graces the National Register of Historic Places. The 128-room hotel is one of the most palatial in the state. Indeed, it was modeled after Italy's Villa Medici and boasts a Florentine fountain in a charming landscaped courtyard. The hotel's renovated beige lobby must be one of the most beautiful in the western United States, the myriad chandeliers, fireplaces, oil paintings and potted palm trees hark back to the days of Royalty and the Very Rich.

The Hotel Colorado was actually financed by the silver mining of the nearby Aspen region and opened officially on June 10, 1893. The cost was a horrendous $850,000; some 16 private railroad cars of the industrial barons drew up on a special Glenwood siding. Leading citizens from all over the world registered. European millionaires arrived in droves to stay and dine here. In 1905, President Theodore Roosevelt brought his own appetite; a typical menu encouraged the presidential visitor and his entourage to consume an eight-course repast:

Caviar Canapes
Consomme Rothschild
Veal Sweetbreads
Young Turkey
Spring Lamb
Broiled Squab
Figs
Roquefort Cheese

To be sure, Roosevelt—an avid bear hunter—made the hotel his Spring White House, complete with direct telegraph connections to Washington and special couriers bringing international news to the hunting head of state.

"The Marvel of Hoteldom" attracted the likes of the Armours of packing house fame, the "Unsinkable" Molly Brown, who managed to survive the Titanic sinking and President William Howard Taft, who appeared for an address of the local populace during his term. World War II transformed the hotel into a naval hospital. In more recent times, moneys were spent to update the facilities, to repair leaking roofs and stalled elevators or failing steam heat. Thanks to their antiques, several suites remind of yesteryear's elegant clientele.

The hotel now offers conference and convention space, a cozy bar, a health club and even an Activities Center for cross-country skiers, golfers, runners and cyclists. The tariff is expensive but in line with a five star hotel.

For more information and reservations: 526 Pine, Glenwood Springs, CO 81601; (303) 945-6511.

Aspen: Redstone Castle

Even by Colorado standards, it is a long and complicated drive—first to Glenwood Springs and then to Carbondale—but the trip is worth it, and the distance only enhances the charms of the little hamlet of Redstone and its historic inn and castle.

You at once see the imposing **Redstone Inn** at the end of the main street. The Tudor clock tower is an unexpected sight in this remote mountain landscape. The 35 rooms seem cozy and unpretentious. Rates are moderate. The lobby and the restaurant are filled with antiques and a Victorian atmosphere.

Now on the National Register of Historic Places, the small Redstone hostelry was built in 1902 for unmarried coal miners. The building had steam heat and even a barber shop. Later, more than $1 million were invested in hotel facilities. A stay here at elevation 7,200 feet means pure air and a true escape from the city. In summer, horses are for rent; trout fishing is popular. The Crystal River is quiet and lovely. Hikers enjoy the area as do backpackers. In winter, the inn serves as headquarters for cross-country skiing.

One and half miles away, you'll see the famous **Redstone Castle**. It began in 1900 as the home of mining baron J. C. Osgood, whose Fuel and Iron Company made him a millionaire. Osgood had extravagant tastes: his $2½ million "Cleveholm Castle" ceilings were covered with gold leaf; his furnishings were embellished with silk brocade and imported ruby velvet. The baronial opulence included elegant chandeliers and expensive Oriental carpets. He built coachman's quarters, a carriage house and elaborate stables.

Osgood's castle has 42 rooms, 14 fireplaces, oak paneling, assorted red turrets, dormers and terraces; it is surrounded by its own golf course and 450 acres of mountain land. Osgood and a succession of wives enjoyed entertaining industrialists and celebrities of his times. Today, you can view the castle from a distance; the rooms are closed to the public except by special arrangement.

The little hamlet of Redstone is idyllic. Just a few houses, some artisan and gift shops, a cafe and a general store.

You reach Redstone via I-70 west to Glenwood Springs, SR 82 south out of Glenwood toward Aspen, turn right at Carbondale on SR 133, 12 miles to Redstone. For more information: The Redstone Inn, Redstone, CO 81623; (303) 963-2526.

Colorado Snowshoeing

The scene is a Saturday morning in Ashcroft, a remote Colorado ghost town near Aspen. The first sunrays redden the snow. The base of nearby Castle Peak is still mauve. Nothing seems to stir in this winter landscape. Then complete daylight, bright, golden, topped by the flawless Colorado sky.

A few human figures assemble down the road from Ashcroft's weather-beaten buildings. Quietly, more people arrive, get together, wait for still others. All carry snowshoes, which will permit an unhurried penetration of this back country.

By 9 a.m. 40 snowshoers stand ready, almost twice as many as the Colorado Mountain Club leader had expected.

Why is old-fashioned snowshoeing in again? The reasons are easy to understand. For one thing, snowshoeing is just winter hiking. You don't need any lessons; you learn to walk with your webbed contraptions in minutes. Age is no factor, and women do just as well as men. Snowshoeing is healthy; that's why you find many doctors devoted to it.

A sports medicine committee of the American Academy of Surgeons made a study of energy output in various sports. According to one of the cardiologists, snowshoeing proved exceptionally good for the heart. The energy expenditure is at a safe level. Besides, you can rest during the trip and survey the scenery. For all ages, this sport means:

- a better workout for heart and lungs
- a better muscle tone
- better-functioning organs
- better digestion
- better circulation

Cardiologists will tell you that leg veins have valves to maintain circulation. Good muscle tone helps squeeze these veins. The valves permit the blood to go one way, back toward the heart. The better the tone of the leg muscles, the better the circulation, the less work the heart has to do. Vigorous use of the legs is important whether it is walking, bicycling, skiing, snowshoeing or any other exercise that uses the legs.

You can go almost anywhere on snowshoes: up the steep winter meadows of the Continental Divide, across the gentle mounds of eastern Colorado, over frozen Lake Dillon, in the deep-snow regions above Silverton and Ouray. In a survey made by the Sierra Club (which has an active snowshoe chapter), some members explained their own special motivations: "We don't disturb nature on snowshoes. We don't upset ecology."

That's what makes the sport different from skiing, especially the kind done at resorts. Colorado's snowshoers demand no cutting of trees, no bulldozing of ski boulevards, no base lodges noisy with hard rock music. Modern ski complexes resemble mechanized cities, with lifts of all kinds, $30 ticket prices, and long lines of waiting customers. By contrast, snowshoers never have to stand in a queue; they can move whenever they please and stay warm in the process. Most skiing is now a status symbol; fashion is absent from snowshoeing. You need only be warm. You can therefore dress in your oldest sweater, the most beat-up windbreaker, a plain cap, an ancient faded sports shirt; no one will judge your income from the pants, either. Any kind of boot will do, including the kind used for hiking.

All this drives down the cost.

Snowshoe equipment is astonishingly reasonable. In a major city like Denver, for instance, you can *rent* a good pair of shoes with harness. What's the charge for the weekend? Between $8 and $12. At an average retail store, you buy a pair of new Canadian snowshoes for a reasonable price.

It's a fairly simple matter to choose a pair of snowshoes. The shape and material may vary, but all of the shoes consist of a frame connected to some lacing. The binding is uncomplicated.

Unless you're in first-rate shape, a first trip will mean some muscle pains. Snowshoes weigh several pounds, and every step means a workout for your legs. As you start out the shoes feel awkward, and it will take 15 minutes until you get used to the wide stance required for walking. (If you step normally, your own legs will be in the way.) You'll eventually learn to raise your feet as little as possible, and after half a mile you won't step on top of your own shoes. But unlike skiing where you must become familiar with the technique, snowshoeing requires mostly good legs. If the snow is right, you can use your leg strength—and body weight—for excellent snowshoe descents.

"The scenic rewards are great," says one enthusiast of the West. "All evidence of man is swept under a deep, sound-absorbing blanket of white. Each pine cone, every spruce branch stand out clearly, Nature is always there."

Planning a Colorado Ski Vacation

The ski lift purrs you upward to 9,000 feet, 10,000, 11,000. At 11,500, you slide off your perch and cross the clearing to a vantage point. You have done it before. But each time you catch your breath. The sight is stunning. The white surface ripples downward to your left and right, agleam in the morning sun. What vastness! Your skis stir impatiently. Is this descent three miles long? Four? More? You can tell from the tiny dots at the bottom—skiers!—that the distance is plenty enough to let you ski to your heart's content.

Suddenly, temptation gets the better of you and you push yourself off in a flash of poles, and shoot down the bowls.

Aspen, Colorado. It could also be Copper Mountain. Or Loveland Basin or Winter Park. Width and breadth is a western trademark.

Colorado! Skiing remains one of the state's major attractions: Colorado has more resorts and ski areas than most other states, east or west.

You tan easiest at these higher altitudes. You find fewer people on those giant mountains that streak up to 13,000 feet in the Rockies. You get more space for yourself, more lifts for your convenience, and a look at more advanced skiers whom you can copy. (The technical level is high.) A skilled skier aims with precision; he/she can zip around a standing novice, can pick his/her way around trees, can jump a knoll without falling. If you become good at it, you can ski as fast or as slow as you please, and still stop at a moment's notice. (That's the secret, of course, the ability to come to a halt.)

Let no one tell you differently: the snow is much, much better in Colorado's Rockies. It is light, fluffy, easy-to-ski snow, the kind that obeys you. (By contrast, Eastern snow means a constant struggle: you must battle ice and more ice). Eastern landscapes are pleasing to the eyes: gentle, wooded hills, white church spires, rolling terrain. Colorado's western landscapes are grandiose. You feel a powerful impact when you look down into the valleys—far, far down—from the Crested Butte sundeck.

The state's ski meccas are justly famous.

None of Colorado's ski resorts look alike; each has its special character made up of a dozen variables. Century-old mining towns like Breckenridge and Crested Butte have been revived. Aspen is immense and complex. Vail is a giant in every way, an American St. Moritz. Winter Park serves vacationers during the week, and young Denverites on weekends. Loveland Basin and Keystone yield good winter days, made up in unequal portions by sun-stroked faces, pure air, a snowscape that tugs and pulls. Colorado's ski slopes seduce the passionate skier, give a great deal, demand little in return. Only the correct motion and concentration.

If you come to this state any time between November and

April, you should try to ski, even if you've never done it before. It is especially enjoyable for children, who see it as a travel experience. To a housewife, a midweek ski day can help banish boredom, help toward a fresh outlook on life, or simply imbue every limb with fresh energy and total health. (For this reason, some Colorado ski areas now cook up special Ladies Days, where women ski at low prices, complete with lessons from a professional instructor and wine parties afterward.)

To a young couple, the excitement of a ski vacation is the total togetherness that can be found by two skiers on a trail; you weave in and out of the trees, jointly cross the shade and the sunlight, sit together on a chairlift and then enjoy the coziness of a lodge or motel. A ski weekend thus means that a couple can get out of the city, and eliminate—for at least a few hours!—all the wordly and workaday cares.

For sedentary folks, this Colorado activity provides a dose of guaranteed well-being. Even if you don't ski well, a few hours of the sport, with its dipping and ducking, the gyrations and deep breathing give a new lease on life. You feel warm, despite outside temperatures. Your circulation works. Your mind is suddenly calmer; even thinking seems improved. Some people have successfully switched from tranquilizers (or pep pills) to winter sports and hikes in summer. On a ski slope, the motion is constant; it demands concentration lest one falls. And it is precisely this concentration that permits no other thoughts. Gone are worries. Only the white, billowing slope counts. You let it unwind under you, following the white band to the best of your ability, and working up an appetite.

A few Sundays of skiing may actually put you in such good condition that an accident is unlikely. If you fall, you do so lightly, and the snow is soft. You need no longer fear stumps buried deeply under the snow. All sorts of machinery manicure the snow surface into a pleasant even field, which begs you to come on down.

In fact, skiing is so easy on the system (and so beneficial to the waistline) that one Vermont cardiologist even suggests it for people over 70. Climbing is no longer necessary. What with many lift contraptions, you are hoisted effortlessly from the valley to the peak, far away from the hurried city.

Most Colorado ski school directors generally agree that the new ski prospect should first try the sport, renting equipment for the first few times. What do you rent? Not ski clothes, generally, but your skis, poles and boots. Try to rent in Denver or in a metropolitan city, where the prices are lower. (Don't wait until you arrive at the ski area itself.) Also keep in mind that rental rates drop after three and more days. To obtain equipment, you need a driver's license or other identification.

Later, as you go on ski outings on several weekends, you'll want to own your personal gear. Start with ski boots; they're the most individual part of your equipment.

Naturally, ski boots must fit well, and only expert personnel can help there. Unless you get a perfect fit, you'll be uncomfortable and unable to handle your skis properly. Boots should be snug, but not tight, and there cannot be pressure anywhere.

How about your skis? It's a good idea to let the shop sales personnel help you with the choice of skis. The salesperson may ask for your height (or judge it), for your weight (or estimate it), for your skiing ability (you can give him the honest dope). He'll want to hear how often the skis will be used and how much is to be spent. The experienced clerk will not pressure anyone into buying the type of skis the customer doesn't need.

How does a beginner learn the fastest? By taking ski lessons. Even the small American ski hills now have a ski school staffed by members of the PSIA (Professional Skiing Instructors of America). These men and women are especially trained, retrained and certified to cope with novices. Instructors now command foolproof techniques to keep you from falling—the beginners dilemma!—and get you on the ski lifts. Start with a half-day lesson, then practice in the afternoon. Lessons are especially crucial when you stand on a pair of skis for the first time! The first day *is* the hardest. You feel awkward with all this strange equipment hanging from your feet. You are a bit like a sea diver who has been asked to walk in his lead boots.

After a day on the slopes, the new skier manages to keep in motion; the skis no longer seem clumsy. You learn to herringbone uphill and to glide down a gentle incline without a spill. The next step is the snowplow, which becomes your brake, and you start toward the first turns. Instructors can help the average person to ski fairly well in about three to four lessons. (It would take you twice as long on your own.)

Let's move to some other practical aspects. Wherever you go, keep in mind that the week between Christmas and New Year's plus Easter vacations are the busiest times for ski resorts. In general, Colorado ski areas are full during the month of March.

So you'll definitely need a reservation. (Send a deposit!) Ski resorts near Denver can be crowded on weekends, meaning that you should also make arrangements for your sleeping quarters beforehand. (Remember that mail is sometimes slow; to save time and get a quick confirmation, it often pays to make a long distance call.) So much for peak periods.

During the remainder of the season—unless it's college vacation time or there is a big ski race—things are a little less hectic.

Most people who ski Colorado try to share some costs. The solution can be a prepackaged Colorado ski vacation, also known as the Ski Week. (Some packages are for only five days or less, however.) Some ski resorts and specialized travel agents sell all-inclusive packages without transportation. You may prefer the package, which can include your (sometimes lower) airfare as well as lodging, meals, daily ground transportation to the slopes, lift passes and some complimentary surprises. A ski deal is practical for travelers who are pressed for time. The package contains all or most of the components for your vacation. A ski package caters to your convenience, eliminating a lot of correspondence.

You might also consider joining an air travel club. Specialized air travel clubs can offer more reasonable rates than commercial carriers because these clubs have fewer overhead expenses. Unlike the regular airlines, air travel clubs shell out little or no money for advertising. To become eligible for their cut-rate flights, you first pay an initiation fee and then annual membership dues. The clubs often own their own jets.

While some of the Ski Weeks are put together and sold by resorts and resort associations, you can further look into a deal from a motel/condo group, or several combined ski areas or a promotion-minded ski lodge.

You can also book your ready-made vacation at a travel agency. Two major benefits: A travel agent doesn't charge for such service. Secondly, an agent can design your ski vacation with the ingredients as you want them. This saves you time and money.

Resort brochures will give you a clue to the amenities at each hotel. A money-conscious skier may want to consider the extras one by one. Perhaps you can live without a color TV on a holiday. Will the hot therapy pool—or the private fireplace—be really necessary? Such extras generally increase the price. Likewise, older skiers may not be interested in the free fondue parties meant for young singles. A single should look for the phrase double occupancy, which could mean that a lone traveler must pay more for the same ski package.

All in all, comparing the various deals saves you money. Keep in mind that all kinds of local budget possibilities may be available. Many of Colorado's supermarkets sell lift tickets at a discount, for instance. And some smaller, promotion-minded ski areas often offer a combination lift ticket and condo at a low price. Likewise, ticket rates go down if you commit yourself to several days.

In larger cities you can also buy a ski holiday through a ski club. Clubs often charter buses or get special airline rates. Clubs also can reserve condominiums at affordable rates.

The choice of a resort matters, too. A giant place with 20 chairlifts will be wasted on the novice. If you select a less in place, you can be at ease in last year's plain sweater or an old parka. Your first ski winter naturally costs less if you can forsake the latest ski fashions. To keep their budgets in line, even good skiers resist the temptation to wear elegant, name-brand ski apparel. You can save the money for the time when you graduate to bigger ski areas.

Remember that the celebrated ski spas always have the highest ski lift prices. When you pay $30 per person per day at the big name, haute couture mecca for lift rides, you've spent a good portion of your budget. You may get the same ski mileage at a lesser known spot for much less. (Agreed: as you become a good skier, you'll want to try Vail or Aspen.)

For overnight stays, ski lodges are most enjoyable (and sociable) if you can afford them. You'll have to pay for the convenience of direct slope access, heated swimming pools, Finnish saunas and Swiss maitre d's. Chic ski lodges are more expensive than hotels or motels, and motels are often more expensive than guest homes or guest houses. The latter can be fine for a ski vacation even if there are no Ping-Pong tables or bars. Condos work out well for large families or large groups.

As an alternative, find yourself a small housekeeping cabin, where you can cook for yourself. Or see if there are farmhouses with rooms for rent to skiers. Young people look for skiers' dorms.

But then, money isn't everything, and on the Colorado ski slopes, democracy shows up nicely. You'll mingle with rich and poor. Skiers are usually in a good mood, and after the day on the hill, you'll feel great. You've pumped your lungs full of that precious fresh air. Your mind is washed clean by the day's silence, which is better for some people than the cannonball noise of the bowling alley. Like the climber, you have been way up there in the quietness of the Colorado mountains, above it all. And you want to go again, soon, soon.

For more information, contact Colorado Ski Country USA, 1410 Grant Street, Denver, CO 80203; (303) 837-0793.

Peach Orchard Harvests in Palisade

Noon at Palisade, Colorado. The golden peach of the sun has already climbed to the top of the trees, which stand out against a poster-blue sky. You've been in the Clark family orchards since seven that morning, up and down the ladders. The guys in Denver's health clubs (pumping iron indoors) should envy you out there in the fresh country air. You've gulped big amounts of it, breathing deeply. No pollution. Your nostrils take in the Elberta peach bouquet.

You reach rhythmically for the warm, ripe fruit, which you plop into a sack hanging from your shoulders. When it's full, it weighs 40 to 50 pounds, enough for the waiting baskets.

Your arms must stretch, your trunk must rotate, you keep bending. Your legs withstand the extra load; you rejoice the climbing and descending from and to the terra firma. In fact, you've gotten your second wind. Despite the heat, you accelerate before lunchtime. The bushels add up. The mood in the orchards is relaxed.

The pleasures of working a peach harvest shouldn't be underestimated. When other people must slave in office cubicles in dirty cities, some folks are outdoors, in the clean, sweet-smelling orchards, getting paid for being in touch with trees and leaves and fruit. This is a pretty world for summer sport, with the colors lingering behind your eyelids for a long time.

At Palisade, on Colorado's Western Slope you're into Elbertas. A collegian from Colorado Springs who has come to Palisade ever since he was a high schooler feels nostalgia about it. He says: "Peach time reminds me of homemade ice cream, or a secret treasure in the lunch box, a tantalizing centerpiece, or even a long drive back from the orchards amid bushels of tree-ripened Elbertas, munching on the way and saving the pits to plant."

Suddenly it's late August, and the 320 growers in Palisade (which is 238 miles west of Denver) must round up some 4,000 harvesters to empty some 500,000 trees. The need is so great at this juncture that the orchardists enlist the help of relatives, transients, hoboes (who arrive on freight trains), high school kids (nearby schools close for the occasion), laborers from Mexico, and university students as well as yearly regulars headed by crew chiefs, who come to Western Colorado for those two weeks.

In Colorado alone, the bounty amounts to some 250,000 bushels. Because almost all the harvesting is still done by hand, it takes an army of people to harvest, sort and crate the peaches. This creates an incredible number of temporary jobs.

Negative aspects? Unless you're in good physical shape, you'll find it hard to scale ladders all day, to stretch your limbs until they ache. The string of your filled harvest sack bites without mercy into your shoulders or neck. You keep lugging 48-pound bushels. The work guarantees to make almost anyone lose weight. But you can't compare it to a tennis game in a breeze. In fact, some orchards—especially in those sun-baked, parched, wrinkled Colorado plateaus—get extremely hot. The canopy of trees is pierced by the sun's rays. Count on sweating a lot. You're only cool at 7 a.m. when you start, and in some parts of the country at 6 p.m. when you finish. (The Palisade Chamber of Commerce crows about the "354 days of sunshine.")

Some comers also forget about the peach fuzz. You won't feel it for a few hours but after a day, it stings. (Some persons are allergic to the fuzz and break out in hives.) Talcum can help the average harvester. But it remains a problem.

Benefits? You can easily make friends, learn about other harvests, get tips on where to split to next. In Palisade, **The Orchard Cafe** is full of beer drinkers at night, hatching plots for the balance of the year and the coming seasons. Colorado peach harvesting is a trip that usually leads to another trip.

From Denver, drive west on I-70 toward Grand Junction until you see the Palisade turnoff.

Colorado Mountain Peaks

The following mountains are Colorado's fourteeners—peaks that are 14,000 feet or higher.

Mt. Elbert 14,433	Mt. Belford 14,197	Humboldt Peak 14,064
Mt. Massive 14,421	Mt. Yale 14,196	Mt. Bierstadt.......14,060
Mt. Harvard 14,420	Crestone Needle ..14,191	Sunlight Peak 14,059
Blanca Peak 14,345	Mt. Bross 14,172	Handies Peak 14,048
LaPlata Peak 14,336	Kit Carson Peak ..14,165	Culebra Peak 14,047
Uncompahgre Pk .14,309	El Diente Peak ...14,159	Mt. Lindsey 14,042
Crestone Peak 14,294	Maroon Peak.....14,156	Little Bear Peak 14,037
Mt. Lincoln 14,286	Tabeguache Mt. ..14,155	Mt. Sherman.......14,036
Grays Peak.......14,270	Mt. Oxford 14,153	Red Cloud Peak 14,034
Mt. Antero.......14,269	Mt. Sneffels......14,150	Pyramid Peak 14,018
Torreys Peak 14,267	Mt. Democrat 14,148	Wilson Peak 14,017
Castle Peak 14,265	Capitol Peak 14,130	Wetterhorn Peak ...14,015
Mt. Evans........14,264	Pikes Peak 14,110	North Maroon Peak 14,014
Quandary Peak ...14,264	Snowmass Peak ..14,092	San Luis Peak 14,014
Longs Peak 14,255	Windom Peak 14,087	Huron Peak........14,005
Mt. Wilson 14,246	Mt. Eolus........14,084	Mt. of the Holy
Mt. Shavano......14,229	Mt. Columbia 14,073	Cross 14,005
Mt. Princeton 14,197	Missouri Mtn 14,067	Sunshine Peak......14,001

Colorado's Northwestern Mountains Via U.S. 40 and Trail Ridge Road

Peaceful Valley

Here's Colorado's only lodge and guest ranch that has its own little mountaintop chapel—an Austrian one with an onion steeple and a big European bell that sounds meal hours. The church was built at a cost of $3 million by Karl Boehm, a former Austrian, in honor of his late father. A gold plaque on the outside of the always open chapel tells us about the dedication and reminds us "to open the eyes and hearts to the beauty and mightiness of His Creation—to all who worship here, may the chapel instill awareness of His Omnipresence."

On Sunday morning, the lodge owners hold church service for guests in the chapel. Year-round weddings are held up there, above a lovely Shangri-La-like valley, amid the trees and meadows. The Boehms—Karl and Mabel—are frankly religious. If you stay at their hostelry for a summer or winter vacation, you'll have to bring your own wine. The Boehms serve no liquor and dislike bars. On the other hand, guests never lock their rooms except at night (Peaceful Valley has no room keys). And the Boehms hire only nonsmokers for their staff.

The **Peaceful Valley Lodge and Guest Ranch** is one of the few such Colorado places that emphasizes the Christian aspects of a vacation. Breakfasts begin with religious place mats that remind us to give thanks, "Bless, O Lord, this food to our use and us to Thy Service and make us ever mindful of the needs of others, Amen."

Wholesome meals are served family-style the year-round; you sit at long tables, which you share with families—most of them from the midwest and practically all repeat customers.

In winter, the Boehms turn their place into a mini–ski resort for cross-country devotees. Most of the guests have never skied, or just a little. But the ambitious tourer can find 60 kilometers (or about 37 miles) of trails. For racing instruction, you must look elsewhere, though.

The chalet-style lodge and its surrounding meadows sit in an 8,600-foot-high valley between Lyons and Estes Park. Unlike some other such cross-country centers, the 110-bed Peaceful Valley resort employs only relaxed, easy-going instructors. Guides are usually available to take the better skiers into the

Chapter 3
Northwestern Mountains via Hwy 40

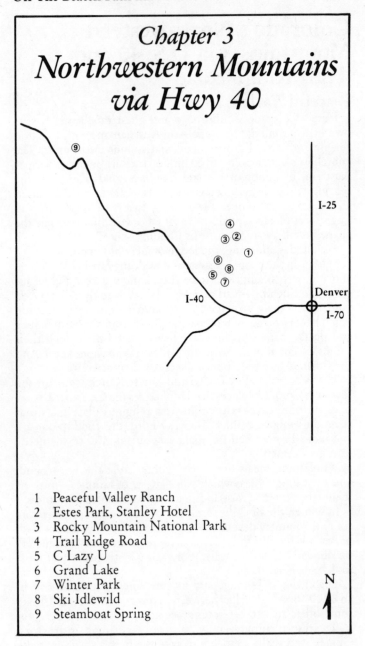

1 Peaceful Valley Ranch
2 Estes Park, Stanley Hotel
3 Rocky Mountain National Park
4 Trail Ridge Road
5 C Lazy U
6 Grand Lake
7 Winter Park
8 Ski Idlewild
9 Steamboat Spring

N

surrounding back country. A week here certainly beats the hectic, expensive, jetset ski resort.

There is a solar-heated indoor pool and hiking trails for people who don't like cross-country skiing. You can play Ping-Pong and watch an occasional movie or a Boehm travelogue at night. Mabel Boehm personally cooks the excellent three meals a day, and she serves the large portions in the comfy knotty-pine dining room. The meals are part of the packages that include ski lessons, too.

In summer, guests enjoy outings on foot and the ranch's own tennis court. Fishing is popular. But the main business then concentrates on dude ranch activities on a large scale, with lots of horses and wranglers and tall Karl Boehm himself giving riding demonstrations. At night, you can get square dance instruction—one of the few such ranches in the United States to offer such lessons. (One warning, though: none of the lodge rooms has a TV.)

The resort's location couldn't be better. It's only 60 miles west of Denver. No passes to cross. Few people. Stars standing out sharply at night. And the Boehms will be the first to tell you that up here you're a little closer to God.

The Peaceful Valley Ranch is located above Lyons, CO 80540; (303) 747-2582. Moderate rates include family-style meals. You get there from Denver via the dramatic Middle St. Vrain SR 7 and SR 72.

Estes Park

On a July day in 1982, a flood roared into one of Colorado's most visited tourist centers. The water raged through Elkhorn Avenue, **Estes Park's** main street, breaking shop windows, causing wholesale destruction. The Fall River rose, tearing into motels and mountain cabins. Four people drowned. The damage was estimated at $31 million. Worse, that season—and part of the next—the flood stopped tourism in its tracks.

Estes Park has been rebuilt by now. The reborn main street offers prettily painted benches, trees and planters, new sidewalks, souvenir stores. A church has become an array of shops. Someone coined the slogan, "The Gutsiest Little Town in Colorado!" Some 250,000 tourists come to stay here each year. They enjoy themselves in a myriad of ways. They flock to the nearby **Rocky Mountain National Park.** They scale the nearby Twin Owl rocks; you can see the climbers in town, hung with hardware, ropes slung across their chest. Other visitors carry fishing tackle; trout is plentiful. (Colorado license required.) Wildlife abounds and the air is pure in the surrounding mountains.

Estes Park has two golf courses, including one that occupies land once owned by the famous Earl of Dunraven, an Irish nobleman who discovered the area in 1827 while on a hunting trip. The American homesteaders followed during the 1870s. Nowadays Estes Park has about 5,000 permanent inhabitants, plus 50,000 others who own mountain cabins and show up briefly in summer, and often keep to themselves.

To be sure, the town is ideal for vacationing families. Estes makes boredom an impossibility. An aerial tram rises to **Prospect Mountain**, a few blocks from Elkhorn Avenue. **Trout Haven**, also close by, features several ponds stocked with rainbows, plus gear for rent. On nearby **Lake Estes**, you discover the headquarters for a white water rafting company. (Full day trips.) Access to family hiking terrain is free and almost unlimited. For those who prefer to do their nature exploration by automobile, a drive along the spectacular 50-mile-long **Trail Ridge Road** is recommended.

The reborn Estes Park presents some contrasts: new and old, serene and loud, natural and artificial. The touristy aspects of the town will disturb the sensitive traveler. Mountains don't seem to suffice. Your children can slide down the Water Tube Express ("340 feet of exciting loops! Video Game area!") or race noisy little Go-Karts ("Grand Prix! Thrilling! A Blast!") On Elkhorn Avenue, a store prints handbills with headlines ("The Smiths having a Ball in Estes!" or "Patsy Saw Her First Snow!!") or sells T-shirts with messages ("Colorado is owned by Canadians").

For all visitors, there are rodeos, parades, chamber music concerts, Rocky Mountain National Park lectures and campfire programs. Still other possibilities: you can shop for Indian crafts or jewelry, for sporting goods, Western wear or mineral specimens.

When should you come to Estes Park? Avoid July and August: Elkhorn Avenue then turns into a tourism circus, with thousands of people descending upon the town. Early June and September are good months. A tranquil time begins after Labor Day.

Accommodations? A good night's sleep is guaranteed at the

well-managed **Longs Peak Inn and Guest Ranch**, with its stables, fishing streams, hiking paths. The **Ponderosa Lodge** overlooks the now peaceful Fall River; some units were damaged by the flood but rebuilt. The **YMCA** in the Rockies rents housekeeping cabins. Estes Park has a **Holiday Inn** with a large indoor swimming pool. The **Stanley Hotel** is the most elegant and historic in town. Except for the moderately priced YMCA, the tariff for *summer* accommodations is expensive.

The trip to Estes is worth your while. The flood is past history now, water under the bridge. The "Gutsiest Little Town in Colorado" thrives again.

Estes Park is 61 miles northwest of Denver, and easy to reach via the Boulder Turnpike and SR 7 from Lyons. For more information, write Estes Park Chamber of Commerce, Estes Park, CO 80517.

Rocky Mountain National Park

Already one hundred years ago, an Englishwoman named Isabella Bird waxed enthusiastic about Colorado's landscape. She came upon the Longs Peak region on horseback. What expressions of wonder! "Exquisite stretches of flowery pastures dotted with trees sloping down-like to bright streams full of red waistcoated trout or running up in soft glades into the dark forest, above which the snow peaks rise," wrote the lady, and the description still fits.

The **Rocky Mountain National Park's** peaks and lakes have present-day names that bear witness to it all: the tourist can view Deer Mountain, Isolation Peak, Snowdrift Peak. Those who come afoot—and more people do every year—may head for Dream Lake, Lone Pine Lake, Fern Lake and up to Chasm Lake.

All belong to the stunning 410-square-mile span of the Rocky Mountain National Park. Established by the federal government in 1915, the park now encompasses 91 upthrusting peaks above 11,000 feet above sea level. Longs Peak is the highest mountain in the Park at 14,256 feet.

The park's assets exceed those of many other national parks. There are more things to do here, yet the expanse also brings happiness to the inactive. Nearby resort hotels are inviting with clean rooms and deck chairs, and the park appeals to the most sedentary motorist.

Nature studies, lectures and tours are conducted by park

rangers. The park's many summer doings make the area especially attractive to tourists. There are not only campfire programs but also a number of short self-guiding nature paths for the benefit of families. (You can bring small children, too.) A Colorado fishing license entitles you to angle for trout in the park's many lakes; some 350 well-marked trails invite the hiker. Wildflowers abound in late spring.

The Rocky Mountain National Park is especially popular with backpackers, who need a permit, and with rock climbers, who must check into park headquarters first. The most difficult climb is Longs Peak Diamond, fit only for elite Alpinists.

The Park Service exacts a small fee to enter the mountainous domain; if you plan on visiting other parks, it will be worth your while to buy a Golden Eagle Passport. It's good for your car and its occupants during the entire year. Travelers aged over 62 years may ask for a (free) Golden Age permit.

Please note that the Rocky Mountain National Park has become so popular during recent years that every year nearly 3 million people stream through each of the three entrances, especially in summer. The major highway, Trail Ridge Road, closes in winter.

Rocky Mountain has only five campgrounds, which is less than a third of Yosemite's or Yellowstone's. No hookups are available for trailers; the big ones, like Airstreams, are hard to navigate in the park. Some tents already go up early in the morning, and at the peak of the season—July through Labor Day—accommodations may be hard to come by even in neighboring towns.

There are several ways to avoid the crowds and still enjoy the Rockies' pleasantly cool summers, the green of pine, spruce, fir, and the mosaic of wildflowers and the water that cascades down those Rockies. For instance, you can arrive early in the season, or after the children are back in school. You can relax by renting a mountain cabin.

Autumn is the best time of all. Coloradans call it Indian Summer; it means a seemingly endless string of clear, warm days. The evenings turn crisp and the nights are chilly, so bring an overcoat. Mid-September seems the best period. Come after Labor Day, and you'll find less competition for the area's good rooms, restaurant tables, traffic lanes.

In winter, a small national park ski area known as Ski Estes Park invites skiers. The ski lifts are modest, however, just T-bars,

Pomas and buses. Cross-country skiing is plentiful. In summers, the patient animal watcher can see deer, elk, sheep, beaver, pikes and many birds as well.

The Englishwoman was right about the park and its "exquisite stretches."

From Denver you can reach this ultrascenic region via several routes. Some summer motorists head west from the Mile High City, cross Berthoud Pass, via U.S. 40 and then arrive in the Rocky Mountain National Park via Grand Lake (altitude 8,369 ft. and icicle-cold). You can also come on the spectacular Peak to Peak Highway (SR 72 and SR 7) from Black Hawk. The drive is especially enjoyable in late fall when the aspen trees burst into gold. Earmark at least half a day to get to the national park via this route. To save time, you can drive through Boulder and Lyons instead (use U.S. 36), it's about 24 miles to Estes Park and the Rocky Mountain National Park gates.

Historic Stanley Hotel

If you happen to come to Estes Park at the high season—and want to be above the melee—you might consider the short uphill drive to the **Stanley Hotel**. It stands up above the busy town like a white castle. The 100-room Stanley reminds you of those old Swiss Grand Hotels—aristocratic, flawlessly kept up, frequently restored, a monument to good taste and good manners. The hotel is all stately white columns, Victorian furniture, fireplaces crackling in the lobby, rooms with impeccable white linen, polished cherrywood furniture and antique dressers. The handwrought leaded glass windows, the spotless white tablecloths in the (deluxe) dining room, the comfortable bar add to a vacation feeling. Miles of walks surround the hostelry, which is at elevation 7,500 feet.

The historical hotel was built by the inventor of the Stanley Steamer automobile. Back in 1905, doctors gave F. O. Stanley, the inventor, only a few months to live. Stanley gathered his wife, her maid and his controversial Steamer and headed for the Colorado Rockies. The undaunted old gentleman was determined to drive his vehicle to Estes Park, Colorado, regardless of roads declared impassable. He victoriously covered the 20-mile stretch in a record one hour and fifty minutes. The inventor suffered from tuberculosis, and his doctor had sent him to Estes Park with the hope of prolonging the patient's life "for a year or so." The sturdy old gentleman was to live for

Famous Stanley Hotel, Estes Park, Colorado

another 37 years. (He reached the age of 91.)

The ingenious, eccentric millionaire ran his lavish hotel facility with a style all his own. In order to bring chamber music to Estes Park for his guests, he had a huge New York Steinway piano shipped to Colorado by ox cart. His resort, located on 160 acres of land, was part of the 6,000-acre Lord Dunraven hunting estate.

Most of the guests arrived by train, to be picked up in Stanley's steaming ten-horsepower automobile. The "all-electric" hotel charged $8 a day, gourmet meals included.

The Stanley Hotel opened in June, 1909. It had cost $1 million to build and was described as "simply palatial." The materials had come by horse teams on roads that Stanley himself designed. A magnificent white edifice with dormers and flagpoles and elegant porches welcomed the hotel guests. Once inside the lobby, the arrivals were dazzled by the hand-carved wooden staircase, the ornate brass elevator, the carpeted halls that led to rooms with lead windows and four-poster beds.

Stanley, who'd made huge sums with the invention of his automobile and later with photo-dry plates, personally designed the hotel's electric kitchens. He ordered the decor of a music room, arranged for a gentlemen's smoking room (even if he never touched tobacco himself) and enjoyed showing up in the billiard room. The legendary Stanley Hotel eventually attracted celebrities such as Theodore Roosevelt, John Philip Sousa, Molly Brown and others.

Remarkably enough, F. O. Stanley's creation still stands, indeed, it prospers. It can be found in the National Register of Historic Places. The music room is still there, as is a writing room. Picture windows and restaurant views give to the mountains including Longs Peak. Tennis and swimming are available in summer. A year-round theatre flourishes; in fact, the hotel stays open through the winters as well. Rates are moderate when the snow falls; summer accommodations are expensive, as they should be at this palace.

A 1906 Stanley Steamer automobile stands in the lobby, as a reminder of how it all began.

Stanley Hotel, P.O. Box 1767, Estes Park, CO 80517; (303) 586-3371. In Colorado: 1-800-ROCKIES.

Trail Ridge Road

Superlatives? Consider **Trail Ridge Road,** in the 414-square-mile Rocky Mountain National Park between the towns of Grand Lake and Estes Park. The road is the highest continuously paved highway in the United States. More? It's one of the highest such connections for automobiles; it allows you to drive for 11 miles above the 11,000-foot level, above timberline, face-to-face with mountain giants that rival those of Switzerland.

The season is short for a visit, though. Deep snows and snow drifts cover Trail Ridge all winter; indeed, the famous road is only open from Memorial Day until the first snowfall, around October 1st. Then everything closes down; Grand Lake and Estes Park are 50 road miles apart.

Dazzling figures: You climb for 4,700 feet on a highway that has serpentines like those of Alpine passes. At one point, you reach the 12,184-foot (3,713-meter) level, where the air is thin and the ultraviolet rays are strong; then you descend to Grand Lake, which is 4,000 feet below. In between, you spot some of Colorado's highest mountain ranges; when you park, you find yourself in view of rock piles deposited here during the Ice Age, known as moraines. There's the Iceberg Lake View at 12,080 feet and a high meadowland known as Tundra, which reminds of Alaska.

Your family can learn much about forestry below timberline: The lovely aspen tree occurs in stands at elevations of about 9,000 to 10,000 feet. Trail Ridge Road also provides a home for alder trees and Douglas fir. In the confier family you find blue spruce, lodgepole pines and the beautiful Pinus ponderosa. At some higher levels, 9,500 feet and up, grow the subalpine fir, lodgepole pine, and the Englemann spruce.

How do you distinguish between the many species of conifers? The differences are noticeable. Spruces, for example, can be identified by cones that stand up straight like candles, and spruce needles are attached singly to the twigs. By contrast, ponderosa pine needles come in clusters of two to three; the bark is a dark brown. Lodgepole pine needles are attached in pairs.

Like most important Colorado highways, Trail Ridge has a long history. First came the Utes and other Indian tribes, who actually followed the already marked trails of wild animals. Miners used it in the 1880s. In 1929, Congress appropriated almost $500,000—a large sum in those days—to build a highway over the Continental Divide. Engineers called it Tombstone Ridge, which became Trail Ridge Road. The paving was finally completed in 1935. The government engineers, normally cool and scientific, became eloquent enough in their final analysis, which mentioned the "deep canyons, many lakes and perpetual snow." The route report concluded: "Below lie streams, valleys, forested slopes, and the realms of civilization. All around are mountains and peaks, no longer towering above but close at hand or seen across some mighty valley."

Travel some 70 miles north and west from Denver (I-25 north to SR 66, west on 66 until it joins U.S. 36) to Estes Park and Trail Ridge Road.

Luxury at C Lazy U

Who has ever heard of a dude ranch with a sauna, two bars, championship tennis courts, racquetball, skeet shooting and golf? Well, there is such a ranch—the **C Lazy U**. It is the only such 150-horse establishment that consistently earns a Five Star Mobil Award or the AAA's (American Automobile Association) Five Diamonds. For good reasons, too. Cocktail hour with hors d'ouevres takes place at the most elegant lounge in this part of the Rockies. Expensive, original oil paintings grace the walls;

later in the evening, there is silver service dining under chandeliers. A pianist plays light music on a Baldwin.

The atmosphere is congenial but slightly formal; gentlemen wear jackets here and you share tables for ten with an international clientele. The steps of the waitresses are muffled by carpets. And never mind the simple, wholesome fare of most Colorado guest ranches. Here, the longtime chef Marion Palmer cooks up Mountain-high stuffed mushrooms as an appetizer, followed by her bouillabaisse soup, turkey crepes, veal scallopini, spinach souffles, Carrots Lyonnaise. Vintage wines flow.

Indeed, the C Lazy U, ensconced in its own Willow Creek Valley some 100 miles west of Denver, is no ordinary guest ranch. You know it at once when you get out of your car and a bellboy takes your luggage and leads you to your plush accommodations. Ah, what thick towels in the bathroom! Oh, is the protein-enriched hairspray, the hand and body lotion, the shower and bath gel, the monogrammed C Lazy U comb all part of the package? It is, along with closets for royalty (which has slept here) and private fireplaces.

At the stables, the wranglers assign you a personal horse for your stay, and you and your group set out into a quiet, slightly remote, truly relaxing 5,000 acres of mountains and hillsides, forests and rivers, ponds and lookout points.

Apart from breakfast cookouts, there are daytime excursions of about one to three hours, some of them meant for novices or softies. Hardier people are often in the saddle for six hours or even longer into the High Country. At night, steak fry outings are popular. (All along, of course, you can take gratis riding lessons.)

To be sure, no one need join *any* equestrian adventures. Fortunately, you can make a C Lazy U vacation as active or as lazy as you wish.

You could, for instance, sit all day around the award-winning swimming pool or test the waters of the huge whirlpool facilities. You could play table tennis on several tables, which are hand-polished every day. You could go on a hike in the luxurious mountain air, far away from the city, with a guide, or *a deux* or alone. C Lazy U can arrange rafting, golfing and tennis lessons. A jogging track is on the grounds. A masseur stands by.

Pond, lake and stream fishing satisfy the most discriminating anglers. Beautiful Willow Creek runs through the ranch for nearly 1½ miles. Professional guides lead you to secret beaver ponds and crystal clear mountain streams.

The C Lazy U offers a competent children's program. Operating between mid-June and Labor Day and again during the Christmas holidays, skilled counselors insure that your youngster is creatively entertained. The little summer guests learn the fundamentals of horsemanship. Even donkey rides are available for the tiny ones.

In winter, the ranch turns into Grandma Moses scenery, all white, with brown barns and fences and the children—colored dots—playing ice hockey, skating and tubing. At the Nordic shop, 100 pairs of cross-country skis and boots and poles await the lucky guests. Some 30 miles of trails are packed and ready; you share these winter woods with elk and deer who show up in the meadows, stealing the horses' hay. You ski in privacy, on the private preserve of George and Virginia Mullin, the C Lazy U owners. When the snow falls the summer's wranglers turn into cross-country guides.

Some guests return every Christmas. C Lazy U then becomes its own little Yuletide world. The holidays are first class, of course. One of the owners says: "On the night of the twenty-third we will have our own big tree-trimming party. Everyone, from the eldest to the youngest, will have an important part in making the big tree beautiful. After dinner on Christmas Eve we will have the presents from the tree, with Santa Claus arriving at the lodge in the little red horse-drawn sleigh with a bag of special gifts for the small children, who also have filled stockings at the large fireplace in the lounge on Christmas morning. On Christmas Day we will have sleighing, ice skating, tubing, horseback riding, skiing, sledding. Brandy milk punch or eggnog is served all through the morning from the big silver bowl in the lounge. Marion has planned delicious menus with everything good that we can possibly think of in connection with Christmas, and for dinner on New Year's Eve we will have our charcoal-roasted prime ribs. There will be the traditional pinata party for the children after dinner, a pizza party for the teenagers, champagne at midnight and a buffet breakfast at one o'clock."

Just who comes to dude ranches like the C Lazy U? You'll probably meet up with some of the Country Western stars, especially those from Tennessee and other southern states. (The south gets hot in summer while the Rocky Mountain West remains cool.) Midwestern farmers enjoy these Colorado vacations. Lately, the Japanese, Arabs and South Americans come, too. European visitors nowadays go in for Colorado's Wild West; Germans often travel fully equipped in riding outfits bought at Western-style stores in Munich or Frankfurt. Because of this ranch's privacy and laid-back style, movie celebrities often use it as a retreat. And the idea also works for honeymooners. (If you ask beforehand, your host's van will be at the Denver airport; cars also pick you up from the train in Granby.)

Apart from celebrities, who stays at the C Lazy U? Lots of very wealthy stock brokers, former governors, army generals. Some millionaires, of course. And according to one horse wrangler, "lots of ordinary people—like lawyers and doctors."

Rates are high and commensurate with the ranch's amenities. C Lazy U is closed in October and November and in April and May. Access: I-70, to Exit 232, along U.S. 40 to SR 125. You'll see the sign. For more information: C Lazy U Ranch, P.O. Box 378B, Granby, CO 80446; (303) 887-3344.

Grand Lake

In August every year, **Grand Lake**—the largest glacial lake in the state—is dotted with sailboats. The marinas fill up with yachtsmen and women. The mountain giants of **Rocky Mountain National Park** lord over the stunning scene. The lake waters are unusually blue. At elevation of almost 8,400 feet above sea level, Grand Lake—lake and community—boasts "the World's Highest Yacht Club." And best of all, Grand Lake is somewhat off the beaten path. You can't get there directly by the famous 13-mile long **Trail Ridge Road**. And U.S. 40 to Denver doesn't connect with Grand Lake, either; you need to come via U.S. 34.

The slightly offbeat location doesn't prevent the international sailing elite from competing here for trophies. Regattas are frequent. The marinas get busy with summer tourists who rent rowboats, paddleboats or motorboats. You see windsurfers. The lake the nearby streams are populated by anglers. Four river rafting companies take you out on various excursions. You have limitless opportunities for hiking. Stables beckon with lots of horses. The surrounding peaks are forested by healthy aspen trees, Ponderosa pine, Douglas fir. You will find waterfalls and mountain flowers.

In winter, the little western town shuts down almost completely; the handsome wooden lakeshore summer homes are abandoned by their rich midwestern and Texas owners; the souvenir shops along the boardwalk shut down. Only a few saloons, a tiny grocery and the pharmacy stay open. Trail Ridge Road is closed. At the same time, the cross-country ski possibilities are plentiful; the Rocky Mountain National Park entrance is only a mile away, and you see skiers even on the golf course. Most winter tourists stay in nearby Granby; the wealthy ones repair to the C Lazy U Ranch.

Grand Lake has lots of summer cabins for rent. Some of the most appealing (but expensive) lodgings are in a series of log cabins known as the **Riverside Guesthouses.** The owners gave nature names to units, like Juniper, Tumbleweed, Alder or Chickadee. Housekeeping rooms and some motels are available, too. The cool air of these elevations appeals to southerners. Rates during the summer season range from moderate to high.

Grand Lake's history is also worth writing about. The Indians called it Spirit Lake. According to local historians, the first Indians arrived around 900 to 1300 A.D. They no doubt stayed during the summer and late fall. Game, fish and other food were plentiful.

The earliest legend of the area tells of Ute, Arapaho and Cheyenne squabbles. Apparently, the Utes living in this summer paradise were suddenly attacked by marauding Cheyennes. Fearing for their women and children, the Ute braves hastily loaded them on rafts and shoved the rafts onto the lake for safety. As the battle with the Cheyennes raged among the trees and along the lakeshore, a storm came up, blowing the rafts far out onto the 400-foot deep lake. The Indians watched helplessly as the rafts were overturned and the women and children drowned. After this time the Utes regarded the lake as dangerous and stayed away, naming it Spirit Lake.

The first white visitors probably showed up in 1855 to hunt for furs and catch the plentiful trout. Although he is best known for his discovery of the Gore Range near Vail, Sir George Gore, the Irish nobleman, also explored the Grand Lake wilderness for a couple of years. He arrived with a party of 50 persons and 30 supply wagons. He brought guides, secretaries, and hunt and fish supply artisans. The country then abounded with game including elk, bear, deer and buffalo.

Other hunters and trappers of lesser stature came next, and

some, attracted by the remote beauty of the area, remained to become the region's first settlers. Among these were Joseph L. Westcott who became the first postmaster of Grand Lake in 1877. Westcott, later known as Judge Westcott, remained here most of his life.

In 1881, the little hamlet of Grand Lake got its first sizable general store, and the Grand Central Hotel was completed. It was a decade of summer residents building homes that looked out on the water. The first big regatta took place here in 1912, on the 12-mile long lake. It is measured only a mile across, so you always see the other shore. The mountain backdrop is as stunning as any in Switzerland.

Take I-70 from Denver until you see the exit to U.S. 40; follow it to Granby, where you reach Grand Lake via U.S. 34. For more information: Grand Lake Area Chamber of Commerce, P.O. Box 57, Grand Lake, CO 80477; (303) 617-3402.

Winter Park Skiing

How does a large ski area come to be? Where did it all start? To understand **Winter Park** and its landscape better, some historical background may be in order.

A few hardy Denverites already skied in the region around 1920. Winter Park (or then West Portal) consisted of sawmills and railroad shanties; a tunnel construction shack served as a warming house to skiers who sought their thrills in forest glades and down logging roads. They climbed the Winter Park hills under their own steam, all the while dreaming of real trails. The dream became a reality in the midthirties when several ski clubs laid out better runs.

Denver's manager of Parks and Improvements was among the first to see the potential. He appropriated the funds for a first ski tow, a T-bar of sorts, built with staves from old whiskey barrels. In March, 1937, the Denver official told an astonished Colorado audience: "We'll create a winter playground unequalled in the world!" He brought in Otto Schniebs, then one of America's most famous skiers. Schniebs, who spoke of the sport as "a way of life," was enthusiastic about the runs.

Winter Park's official dedication took place on Jan. 28, 1940. A ski band played. Hans Hauser, a handsome ski school director, had been commandeered from Austria. Alf Engen, the jumper, came from Utah to show his stuff. A ticket for the half-mile-long lift cost one dollar (50 cents for students).

By 1947, Winter Park (which got its name from its designation as a winter park in Denver's Park System) had three T-bar lifts and four rope tows. Owned by the city of Denver, the area made good progress during the early fifties; soon there were numerous chairlifts, which multiplied every season. (The area now has 14 lifts.)

The history of this ski mecca was crowned in 1975 when its capacity was almost doubled. To drum up $6 million for lift construction and base facilities seems an even greater feat when you consider the tight money situation of the early seventies.

Twin factors—fairly easy access and adequate accommodations—always helped Winter Park's cause. A Ski Weeker requires no car at this destination resort. To cut costs, many families come directly from Stapleton International Airport via a special daily express bus.

To be sure, Winter Park always attracted Ski Week customers of every age and ability. The slopes are well groomed. The lifts run without fail. A large ski school teaches beginners in record time; three days of lessons should get you up and down most slopes. The area boasts more than a hundred ski runs that satisfy the most fanatic racer and the rank novice.

Winter Park vies with Colorado's top resorts. Yet it has none of the poshness, the celebrity parade, the hectic atmosphere of other international ski resorts, the wild night life of the Beautiful People. The resort works out well for nonskiers also. Winter Park's managers make it possible for anyone to reach the Mary Jane summit (elevation 12,025) in comfortable, heated vehicles called Sprites. For a few dollars, a vacationer can thus mingle with the fast downhill crowd, take pictures of the deep sunflecked woods, and lunch al fresco at the **Snoasis Restaurant**. Several ski lodges offer heated swimming pools, and even older persons like to spend a few unstrenuous hours on light cross-country skis.

Sleigh rides are available in the evenings. The families climb aboard, snuggle under warm blankets, breathe the forest air, listen to the sleigh bells and to the crunch of snow. Along the way, there will be hot chocolate for the kids, hot spiced wine for adults. In the same Colorado valley, at the same time, vacationers enjoy themselves on a lighted hill, slithering down the slopes on snow tubes.

The 67-mile drive across Berthoud Pass to Winter Park won't take much longer than two hours on I-70 and U.S. 40. The roads are kept sanded.

Winter Park Condo Retreats

Reveille to a winter morning in the Colorado Ski Country. Outside your windows, the sun slants through the conifers; from the condo, cross-country ski tracks take off for the snow-covered forest. You're on the quiet edge of the town of Winter Park. You gratefully set out, skiing through light and shade, breathing deeply. Ah, to be alive! To be in motion!

Later, you return to the comfortable condominium for lunch. Some people are unaware that they can rent these vacation apartments for a night or a weekend, solo, coupled, or as a family of six. Tina Harris, one of the managers at the **Beaver Village Condos**, puts it this way: "Your time with us will be special. You can cross-country ski outside your door or catch a free shuttle to Winter Park's downhill runs. Afterward, you can sit in our sauna, enjoy a jacuzzi, or swim in the indoor pool. It's all included."

Beaver Village is typical for Colorado's condo goodies: a well-equipped kitchen, matching dishes, pots and pans, ironed sheets, clean towels, shiny glassware, cozy generous furniture in earth colors. The 165 units contain moss-covered fireplaces, plus wood. And each *room* has its own thermostat. Tina Harris hands honeymooners a gratis bottle of vintage wine. The Beaver Village Condominiums are managed by Preferred Properties. Reservations at P.O. Box 3154, Winter Park, CO 80482; (303) 726-8813.

At the west end of town, the somewhat larger **Hi Country Haus** complex is tucked away among the trees on both sides of the Fraser River. This is more than a house, of course, but a 306-condo resort in its own right, complete with recreation center, a glass palace full of hot tubs, a grocery store, buses to take you to the Winter Park and Mary Jane lifts, and even private cross-country trails that connect with Idlewild's touring terrain.

The Hi Country Haus condos run true to form: fine kitchen cabinetry, microwave ovens, dishwashers, beamed living room ceilings. Dave Smith, one of the longtime executives uses the slogan, "We're a home away from home." Most of the staff, including President Mike Dybicz, have been here for many years; they know how to run a vacation community.

This is Winter Park's oldest and largest condo complex, and Hi Country Haus service is rapid. Example? You can't seem to get a certain channel on your TV. You call the office; almost at once, the TV repairman shows up to fix the problem. Size doesn't mean impersonality here; some of the units certainly reflect the owners. In Unit #1501, for instance, the coffee mugs come with personal greetings:

My best to you
Each Day
My best for you
Each Day

For reservations: Hi Country Haus Condominiums, Box 3095, Winter Park, CO 80482; (303) 726-9421. The set up is ideal for groups and Dave Smith gets lots of them.

If you want something a little more secluded, more private, you might consider the **Creekside-at-Winter-Park.** These 18 luxurious units come with vistas of Vasquez Creek, its white-pillowed banks and a charming little gazebo. Private balconies look out upon a thick forest of lodgepole pines; one of the region's most idyllic cross-country ski trails starts a few steps from here. Creekside offers covered parking, cable TV, top-of-the-line appliances, deluxe bathrooms with whirlpools, maid service, a free shuttle bus to town and the ski area. Most of all, though, these two- and three-bedroom units are away from the melee and are ultraquiet. For information contact Kenneth McLean at Box 1265, Winter Park, CO 80482; (303) 726-5557. McLean also manages seventy other properties, some of them with endearing names like **Tall Pines, Timber Ridge** or **Sun Song.** Some of McLean's best units even come with hot tubs.

All in all, Winter Park has a remarkable array of condo accommodations. In your search, you'll come upon the unexpected. A complex with racquetball/handball courts? The **Snowblaze Condos** will fill the bill. Grand Hotel-style turndown service at night and fresh flowers in the morning? Try **Destinations West.** A ski-in, slopeside location? Sure, the **Iron Horse Retreat** has it.

And how much does it all cost? The rates at the biggies—the Hi Country Haus and Beaver Village—are typical for Winter Park and all the above listings. On the other hand, on the average, you pay less per night for a condo than you would pay for a hotel room, *providing that you travel with a family or in a group.* Condominiums are a good deal then, especially if you consider the advantages: lots of space, reasonably priced homecooked meals, pretty forest views, and at Winter Park, your own cross-country ski trails.

The Handicapped Can Ski Too

Several times each winter, a most unique ski race takes place in Winter Park, Colorado. The slopes of this giant area are alive with multicolored pairs of flags, and through these gates, at intervals, there descend a succession of skiers. In a downhill race, they're clocked at 50 miles an hour.

Nothing unusual? Not for the ordinary ski racer. But these people are not ordinary. Many of the competitors have only one leg. Others have only one arm or no hands. The rest fly down the Colorado mountain despite paralyzed joints, missing kneecaps, absent toes or stiffened backs.

The skiers are all physically handicapped, the result of disease, accidents or their conditions at birth.

Yet these people show that you can conquer almost any barrier. Eyes shining, cheeks glowing, the racers speed through the finish line.

Colorado's Winter Park Ski Resort actually offers the world's largest teaching program for handicapped skiers. Some 600 volunteer and 15 professional instructors participate in it. Each ski season thousands of lessons are given here to people with cerebral palsy, spina bifida, polio, multiple sclerosis and paraplegia. Some of the students are even blind.

Skiing requires perfect coordination and a good balance. To hurtle down a snowy slope, a two-legged sighted skier uses all his God-given limbs—his feet to direct the two skis, his hands and arms to hold the poles, which act as stabilizers.

The loss of an arm throws the body out of kilter. With only one ski pole, it's more difficult to make the turns or to walk up a hill. Yet when there's a will, there's a way, and practice and determination will make a one-armed skier as good as a two-armed one.

The sudden loss of a leg is more serious, yet even that loss can be overcome. At first, there will be pain; and when the stump has healed, the person will feel off-balance. Then come the weeks of learning the use of crutches. The amputee must strengthen the remaining leg and how the muscles will ache for a while. There's also the self-consciousness. But only at first.

A positive mental attitude will put the handicapped person into the right track within a few weeks. The individual realizes that one can do many things with an incomplete body. Winter Park simply calls it "rehabilitation through recreation." The students themselves often see it as a lark. "Skiing on one leg is

Handicapped Skier, Winter Park

easier than on two," chuckles one participant. "The trouble with *two* skis is that they don't go in the same direction for the beginner!"

The Colorado Handicap Program started in 1970 and has become the largest of its kind in the world. The program began with 23 amputees from Denver's Children's Hospital and each year new disabilities were added. Most of the students now are adults. One of the highlights has been the introduction of the Arroya, a sledlike device used by paraplegics or any individual confined to a wheelchair.

Handicapped skiers with one good leg and two usable arms are taught the three-tracking technique, which means skiing with small outriggers. The outriggers consist of a ski tip attached to the bottom of a modified crutch. In full gear, the three-tracker has contact with the snow on the bottom of the full length ski and balances with both ski tips. In due time, amputee skiers become so proficient that they can enter races.

How is it possible to teach skiing to the blind? In some countries, instructors ring a little bell at every dip of a mountain. Winter Park has used bamboo poles that link instructor and pupil; the key teaching elements, however, are touch and verbal contact. The blind individual has to begin from the beginning: he/she has to learn all about ski boots (and how to put them on) and then about the skis themselves. The feeling of standing on skis comes next, with the feet parallel to one another, then walking to the sound of the instructor's ski poles tapping.

Next, the sightless skier sidesteps up a small slope, constantly in communication with his instructor. Chairlift loading has to be taught, too. Again, with proper instruction and good communication, it proves to be no problem.

The blind person eventually moves on to steered turns, parallel turns, and finally mogul skiing. Oftentimes a sightless skier will progress down the hill to the sound of the instructor calling "turn, turn, turn!" In due time, a close bond develops between the student and instructor.

How is this large Colorado program financed? Funds come from general donations, program fees, grants from private corporations and foundations and special events. The handicapped also pay a small daily fee toward lessons and equipment rental.

The learning experience isn't too difficult for athletic individuals who already skied before injury or illness hit them. Thanks to the use of special gear, people can now take up skiing despite physical problems.

One good example is Larry Kunz, who was born with a spina bifida condition that gave him little muscle control from the knees down. Thanks to Denver's Children's Hospital, Larry was introduced to Hal O'Leary, the Winter Park coach who specializes in the physically impaired. "At first Larry couldn't even walk," O'Leary says. "But in a week, he was able to use his crutch skis and get around in heavy ski boots. Today, he soars down the slopes despite his spina bifida."

Some of the most exciting moments occur on the race course. At one competition, a Winter Park official handed out trophies to the three fastest skiers. "You three won this slalom," he said. "But actually, all you people were winners. You won over your handicap."

More information on the Handicap Program may be obtained by calling or writing Winter Park Handicap Program, P.O. Box 36, Winter Park, CO 80482; (303) 726-5514.

Ski Idlewild

Honestly now, did you ever dream of a family ski vacation yet not dared to go because the resorts all seemed too big, too famous, too overrun, too expensive?

Hesitate no longer. Small can be beautiful, too. And to the novice skier less can indeed be more.

Case in point? **Ski Idlewild**, a miniresort three miles west of Winter Park. Idlewild caters to the person who has never skied before, and to the "little bit" skier. The slopes are so gentle that they remind one more of the midwest than of the rugged Rockies. The total vertical rise amounts to a mere 400 feet. The runs—four in number!—are almost ridiculously short, and the terrain is so wide that it cannot arouse anxieties in even the most timid of first-timers.

Families love the place, of course. No one can get lost; there is only one chairlift plus a short Poma lift. Simplicity!

Says the ski school director, "Beginners *need* to have a good time. That's what we specialize in."

This philosophy also goes for Idlewild's cross-country skiing program. It aims almost exclusively at those who have never stood on the thin, wooden Nordic cross-country skis before. You learn to use them within a few hours. Your guide takes you up into Idlewild's conifer forests. The landscape here is kindly, too. And your guide-teacher will often stop to point out the tracks of deer, ermine or snowshoe rabbits. The trails reflect the character of this country. You tour along a "Winterwoods" trail and descend a "Serendipity" path. Cross-country headquarters are situated in an old red barn, which serves as dude ranch headquarters in summer. The barn stands amid lovely meadows flanked by frozen ponds and a little river. The scenery is relaxing. Someone actually suggested that Idlewild change its name to "Idyllwild." Perhaps so; you're off the highway, away from the thunder of trucks and the caravan of cars. You can park yours here and forget it.

The Ski Idlewild setup includes accommodations at the nearby Hi Country Haus Condos.

After supper, enjoy the sleigh rides, excursions to a nearby lighted tubing hill. It's all fairly low-key and informal.

Ski Idlewild is 69 miles west of Denver via I-70 and U.S. 40. The lifts sometimes shut down at unexpected hours. Call (303) 726-5564 before you come.

Young Winter Park, Colorado ski jumper

Winter Park's School for Jumpers

High up, the ski jumper pushes off, sinks into a crouch, chest tight against his knees. He accelerates in the two steep snow grooves toward the platform. Suddenly, his body uncoils, straightens, dives upward. He is airborne. Seconds tick away. The spectators gasp. Still he soars through the Colorado sky, then a smooth landing. Judges note the distance. The audience roars.

Ski jumping is sensational to watch. Especially in this case.

The competitor was six years old! And his leap was the result of a unique school for youngsters at Winter Park, Colorado, a ski area 67 miles west of Denver. For the past several decades, thousands of kids have been trained here at **Junior Jumping School** in human aviation. Children begin training at the age of six. The upper limit for competitors is 18. And every season, a few lads are so enthused about the program that they bring their little sisters. Even middle-aged fathers have turned up for lessons. And why not? The school is for first-timers. There is a small charge to enroll on a regular basis. Anyone from any

91

state is welcome to take advantage of it. Come to this Christmas tree country any Saturday and Sunday during the entire ski season for all or parts of the program. You can talk to the instructors.

The Winter Park Recreational Association, which runs the popular Winter Park ski area foots most of the bill for this sport. All jumping coaches are adults.

During the season's first get-together, anxious parents ask: could a child come to harm here? Ski jumping is actually much safer than downhill skiing. For one thing, the special hills are well prepared. For another, you jump in a straight line, and training is worked out with great care. No person therefore ever suffered a serious accident at this Colorado school.

Before being taken on, a youngster must know how to ski at least a little. The instructor gives a brief test for this purpose. Then he groups his pupils by age. Class I is for 16–18-year-olds; Class II includes ages 14 and 15; Class III, 12 and 13; Class IV, the 9–11-year-olds; and Class V, under nine. All are taught separately. Fortunately, Winter Park's Junior Jumping School is lighthearted enough for an occasional snowball fight, and there are neither roll calls nor other regimentation.

How do you create a young ski jumper? The novices first learn the basic aerodynamic position for the inrun, meaning the short chute spurt before takeoff. They're taught the precise instant for leaping. They're shown how to stop safely and gracefully. In between are various exercises. When the young-sters are ready to make actual jumps, they always start with the smallest hills. You only fly for a few feet here, but you get an idea of what it's like. A few tyros may at first have their hearts in their throats. After a single leap, though, the kids like the flight so much that they come back for more. Dropouts are rare. Most of the little jumpers feel like conquerors. "I'm a pilot!" they cry. "I'm a bird!" "Look at me! I'm a kite!"

A few jumps later, you graduate to bigger hills, where you can zoom 30, 40 or more feet. In all, Winter Park has seven jumping installations. The largest, which is only for teenagers, allows distances of 200 feet; here speeds of 55 MPH are normal. In addition to coaching, Winter Park arranges for at least six competitions on every jumping hill. And from time to time, the winners battle it out at other Colorado ski areas as well. To be sent to Steamboat Springs or Summit County is a great honor, of course.

The jumping meets pack the greatest excitement, both for the young athletes and for the spectators. The eager freckled faces, the colorful sweaters, the splashes of reds, greens and blues of parkas and ski pants and caps are a delightful sight. Before each leap, tension fills the thin, sweet mountain air. Up on top, the eyes squint under big goggles. Boys get last-minute advice from instructors. Five-year-olds wonder: Will they jump far enough? Will they look good enough in the air? Will they beat the competition?

These junior affairs are staged much like adult champion-ships: The boys wear bibs with starting numbers. The reporters are there; the ski patrol stands by in case of the rare sprain; the judges sit sternly in a tower, ready to compute results. The jumpers are not only judged by what distances they can reach, but also by their style. They lose points, for instance, by standing straight after takeoff. (The jumper must be forward while in flight.) They lose points if their skis flutter in all directions. (The skis must be together.) They cannot win if their arms go like windmills. And they're evaluated for their landing—which should be steady—and for the ease of coming to a halt (no hands).

This is the real thing, and even the tiniest of the 90 to 200 youngsters try to do their best. Afterward, the kids get ribbons, and the year's final championship means a trophy for at least one jumper. Fortunately, even the losers receive a prize; it's a school shoulder patch for their parkas. You'll see moppets wearing this insignia with great pride.

Some of the jumpers keep training until the sun goes down behind the darkened fir trees. The youngsters struggle upward to fling themselves into the sky, soaring and soaring. At a time when we're often told that the American youth is going soft, Winter Park must command attention. Soft? The fresh, scrubbed, entrancing faces may look it. But after one or two winters, these leaping lads become as hard as the steel edges under their skis. Surely, some of them will do us proud in a future Olympics!

Winter Park Recreational Association, P.O. Box 36, Winter Park, CO 80482; (303) 726-5514.

Steamboat Springs
In 1875, James Crawford, the first white settler of **Steamboat Springs,** arrived here from Missouri with two wagons, his

family, his horses and a few head of cattle. He was attracted to the area by a newspaper article. The author of the piece described his view from the top of the Park Mountain Range as "a wilderness of mountain peaks and beautiful valleys, dark forests and silvery streams—a deserted land except for immense herds of elk and deer and buffalo which had not yet learned by experience to shun the presence of man."

The Yampa Valley's idyllic setting and mild climate made the eventual "presence of man" inevitable. Even before Crawford built his log cabin along the west bank of Soda Creek, the Yampa Valley had sheltered the Ute Indians and later French and English fur trappers. (Legend has it that French fur trappers named the town Steamboat Springs because of the peculiar chugging sound from the hot springs near the river.)

Cattle ranchers had found Steamboat's emerald green slopes ideal for fattening their herds en route to market. Hot and cold running water in the forms of three creeks, numerous hot springs, and the flow of the Yampa River lured more and more settlers to the valley.

Recreational skiing first came to Steamboat in the early 1900s when Norwegian Carl Howelson introduced the sports of ski jumping and ski racing to the community.

They've skied in "Ski Town USA" facing Main Street before the turn of the century on long boards, with a long staff, the women in long skirts. They've jumped here from a giant hill before many other people thought of such things. For years, they've taught Steamboat youngsters to ski, gratis, from kindergarten up, all through high school, and through the small local college. Men with first names like Alf, Ansten, Lars or Ragnar showed off their telemarks turns way back when, and Steamboat Springs skiers—immigrants as well as natives—showed the world what they were made of. Many Olympians cut their ski teeth here.

Steamboat has an excellent ski school, of course, which operates two miles away on Mount Werner. But it also has a Ski Club, and even a Ski Marching Band. The latter unfurls every February oompah-oompah during the **Steamboat Springs Winter Carnival,** one of the country's oldest ski festivals. It features ski-joring and ski obstacle races and ski jumping and skiing with torches and ski parades and ski balls.

At last, in the 1960s, the town was discovered by tourism, first by a giant Texas conglomerate, then by some private investors. In 1981, the real boom began with a Sheraton Convention Hotel.

Millions of dollars have since been invested in new ski lifts, new trails and in reshaping old ones, and other amenities. A Swiss gondola's six passenger car carries loads of skiers an hour up Thunderhead Mountain.

While downhill skiing is taught on a big scale here, cross-country skiing isn't neglected. Sven Wiik, the Swede who owns and runs the **Scandinavian Lodge**, also happens to be a former Olympic team captain and coach of collegiate cross-country races. Fortunately, he is also dedicated to the average Colorado outdoors person, who can learn and perfect the cross-country steps at this well-known Steamboat Springs enclave.

Wiik starts you out on a track where he teaches the right glide; in the afternoon, you're off on the tame paths around the lodge. If Wiik and his experienced instructors consider you good enough, you'll be taken on a tour of Rabbit Ears Pass. Here, you climb and descend through stately conifers.

The Scandinavian Lodge offers lessons already in mid-November, followed by Thanksgiving Touring Clinics. His many programs even include a Citizens Cross-country Race Camp for would-be competitors, many of them in their fifties and sixties.

The lodge itself is a marvel in stone and cedar, with big balconies outside and Danish furniture inside. Wiik has his own little ski shop here, too. Another building contains a complete athletic center, gymnasium and all. The Scandinavian Lodge has expensive rates, which seem commensurate with its facilities and prestige.

Though Steamboat Springs has grown over the years (permanent year-round population is now 6,000), it has retained its scenic beauty and Western charm. Cattle ranching is still important, too. Lots of saddles and boots and Stetsons are for sale in downtown Steamboat.

Those who come to visit or stay are drawn to many of the same qualities that caused James Crawford to settle in the valley.

Steamboat Springs is 170 miles west of Denver via U.S. 40. For information on year-round Steamboat Springs, write or call: Steamboat Springs Chamber/Resort Association, Steamboat Springs, CO 80477; (303) 879-0740.

Southern Colorado
Mountain Driving

Contrary to rumors, mountain driving is not especially dangerous or tricky. According to the Colorado State Patrol, most accidents actually happen in the flat, straight stretches at high speeds.

But the stranger to winter is better off by knowing a few special driving precautions and tricks. Hence, some thoughts are in order here:

• When renting a car in winter, insist on special snow tires, even if the pavement is dry. Also, better to carry tire chains unnecessarily than to be caught without them when they are esssential. Front wheel drive is preferable for better traction.

• Before starting out on any extended trip in wintertime, the following safety equipment should be checked: brakes, headlights and taillights, exhaust system, windshield wipers, defrosters, heaters and tools.

• Starting slowly on snow provides better traction and prevents spinning of wheels or skidding sideways into parked cars or other vehicles or objects. On a slick surface, start in second gear; this keeps the car's wheels from spinning.

• When driving in a fog or snowstorm you get better visibility by using the lower headlight beam. The upper headlight beam tends to reflect back off the fog and blind you.

• Whenever visibility becomes so poor, due to fog or snow, that it is impossible to see more than a few feet ahead, you best pull off the road. Clean the windshield or wait until the weather eases up.

• Car heaters draw in fresh air from the outside. Cars should never be parked directly behind another car that has the motor running.

• When roads are wet and the temperature drops to 32 degrees or below, the surface will become icy. Extreme caution is indicated. A single driver can start a chain of mass collisions on ice.

• Get the feel of the road when pavements are slippery by trying brakes occasionally while driving slowly and away from traffic.

• As the temperature rises, ice (and, to a lesser degree, snow) becomes much slicker. For example, at 20 MPH when the temperature is 32 degees, stopping distance on ice without tire chains or snow tires is 250 feet. When the temperature is at

Chapter 4
Southern Colorado

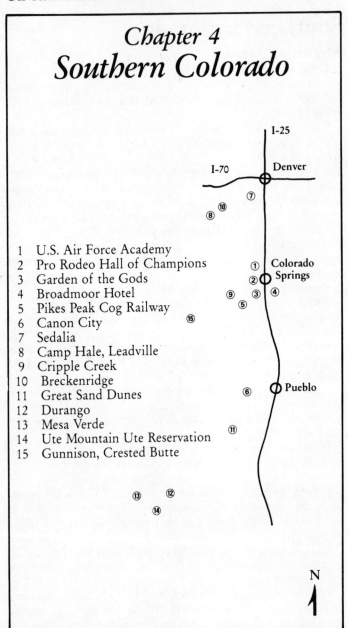

1 U.S. Air Force Academy
2 Pro Rodeo Hall of Champions
3 Garden of the Gods
4 Broadmoor Hotel
5 Pikes Peak Cog Railway
6 Canon City
7 Sedalia
8 Camp Hale, Leadville
9 Cripple Creek
10 Breckenridge
11 Great Sand Dunes
12 Durango
13 Mesa Verde
14 Ute Mountain Ute Reservation
15 Gunnison, Crested Butte

zero, stopping distance is 110 feet. The difference of 140 feet might well cause a serious accident.

• By stopping slowly the driver can prevent skidding and come to a safer halt. If your vehicle starts to skid or the wheels lock, release the brake pressure. Pump the brakes; that is, apply the brakes lightly and *intermittently*. A minimum of pressure should be used. Steady, even braking does the trick.

• Keep your windshield and windows clear, making sure you can see danger in time to avoid trouble. Windshield wiper blades should not be too worn; they should be up to the task of removing rain or snow without streaking. Also, the defroster should function efficiently. Assure good visibility in the rear by removing the snow and ice from the back window when necessary.

• Occasionally a patch of ice will remain on a curve or other shaded spot after the rest of the road has cleared. Be on the lookout for these ice patches.

• A thorough check of the exhaust system should be made at regular intervals; possible leaks could cause a tragedy. (Carbon monoxide poisoning is a deadly driving hazard during wintertime.) It is a good idea to leave at least one window open when driving in cold weather.

• Weather and road conditions in Colorado's mountains are subject to abrupt changes. It is possible to get a report that a certain area is clear, yet you arrive there two or three hours later to find a snowstorm in progress or the highways icy and snow-covered. The reverse is also true and adverse weather conditions often clear up in a short time.

The U.S. Air Force Academy

In all of North America, there is only one **Air Force Academy.** You'll find it 11 miles north of Colorado Springs. It is open to the public; indeed, the Academy is Colorado's most visited man-made tourist attraction. For good reasons, too: much of the architecture is extraordinary, the landscaping handsome, the buildings neatly tucked away among 18,000 acres of pine, spruce and fir forests. Behind the academy rises the impressive Ramparts Range.

Earmark at least half a day for your (gratis) visit. Come by car. Begin at the Visitor's Center off I-25 and get your bearings. The free map will be helpful; it tells you what to see on your 13.5-mile self-guided tour. Although more than one million tourists visit these grounds every year, the property is so

Women are nowadays accepted at the U.S. Air Force Academy in Colorado Springs

spacious—and has so many possibilities for quiet contemplation—that you'll never feel hemmed in.

You'll discover charming picnic grounds, exciting glider takeoffs and landings, a stunning cadet parade (weekdays at noon), complete with marching band. Visitors are welcome to the superbly run 560,000-volume library and to the planetarium, which offers periodic free shows and doubles as classroom for astronomy, physics and navigation classes.

Which is the most popular academy attraction?

It's the 150-foot high Air Force Chapel with its 17 spires—an all-faith church that gives even the nonreligious some aesthetic jolts. The deft use of glass, steel and aluminum, the lead windows and tastefully designed interiors are all memorable. The chapel is unique because Protestant, Catholic and Jewish services can be held simultaneously, and the three congregations can enter and leave without disturbing each other. The Protestant nave seats 1,200, the Catholic nave 500, and the Jewish synagogue 100 worshippers. (The Academy employs a full-time rabbi.) In addition, there is a meeting room for the use of any religious organization that doesn't want to use the three chapels.

The Protestant nave is above the terrace level, a broad flight of steps leading to the vestibule. Stained glass panels suffuse the room with multicolored light. Behind the altar is a curved 14-foot wall covered with pastel shades of glass tessera. The top of the Holy Table, 15 feet long, is a single slab of marble.

The architecturally bold chapel is part of a 75-minute walking tour—a summer feature that the visitor shouldn't miss. The stroll includes numerous other buildings, all of them well conceived and blending into the scenery. Apart from the daily parades of the 4,000 spic and span cadets (including 11 percent females), you can watch periodic air shows, and see a 30-minute introductory film. If you happen to be here in June you may witness the graduating ceremonies. Hats fly into the air then. Newly minted Air Force officers are at last ready for their careers.

You gain a better understanding of the U.S. Air Force Academy when you learn a little about the painstaking selection process and the tough physical and scholastic training.

Only the healthiest, sturdiest, most intelligent and most stable young people are admitted to this school. In most cases a candidate must find a member of Congress to nominate him or her many months before admission. A student must score

Protestant service at U.S. Air Force Academy

high at college entrance exams. There are tough health exams, and the applicant undergoes a hard physical qualification test. For every cadet who is accepted, many more are turned down. (Of 12,000 men and women who apply only about 1,400 will make it.) Many of the rejects are brilliant young people and often high school football heroes.

Once accepted, cadets put in four years of more, wider, and deeper studies than at most universities. In all, they take 145 semester hours of math, civil engineering, computer science, chemistry, physics, physiology, navigation, astromony, as well as English, philosophy and foreign languages, including Russian and Chinese. (The faculty consists of almost 600 professors and instructors, including many career Air Force Officers.)

The hardest time for cadets is the first eight weeks. The newcomer is cut off from the world. Colorado Springs, Colorado, is only a few miles away, yet the cadet receives no pass. He or she is not allowed to drive an automobile. Parents cannot visit.

They'd be amazed if they saw their son or daughter now.

The cadet is up at 6 a.m., then races through the day on the double, doing pushups, sit-ups, chin-ups, sprinting over hurdles.

Inside the gleaming academy buildings, the future Air Force

Classroom, Air Force Academy, Colorado Springs

officer must walk at attention and come to attention before each meal. Actually, the Air Force Academy is tougher than West Point or Annapolis. For one thing, the air in Colorado is thin. Most flatland recruits must get used to the 7,000-foot altitude. So they'll be huffing and puffing at their first calisthenics.

The visitor has a much easier time, and no cause to hurry or march. Vast parking lots are well distributed among the buildings and sport facilities. Cafeterias (and even an Officers Club) beckon for reasonably priced lunches.

Later, you will long recall the wide open spaces, the green healthy grass and multitude of trees, the steep chapel spires, and the blue Colorado sky overhead.

Academy grounds are open to the public the year-round from 6 a.m.–7 p.m. Many buildings open at 9 a.m. and close at 5 p.m. For more information, write: U.S. Air Force Academy, Colorado Springs, CO 80840; (303) 472-2555.

Prorodeo Hall of Champions

What? A *cowboy* museum? A museum with a rodeo theme? Yep, indeed, and it's a sizeable one—a concept you won't encounter anywhere else in Colorado but in Colorado Springs, not far from the U.S. Air Force Academy and off the same I-25 highway.

The cowboy played a vital role in opening the West to the expansion of the nineteenth century, and his reputation for courage and individualism has become part of our national folklore and has shaped our character as Americans.

The **Prorodeo Hall of Champions and Museum** presents this unique heritage in a facility that is both entertaining and educational.

This makes it a fine family destination. The museum offers an outdoor corral with live animals, which always delights children. Inside, you learn a lot through dioramas and exhibits of well-displayed saddles, boots, buckles, spurs, ropes, chaps, branding equipment and other paraphernalia. Rodeo as a sport comes alive through the histories and mementoes of America's major rodeo champions.

The visitor can learn about such colorful rodeo champs as bull rider Warren G. "Freckles" Brown, the oldest man in Prorodeo history to win a riding event. His long career was interrupted by a broken neck as well as by World War II. With typical spirit during wartime parachute jumps into China, Brown put on a rodeo using army mules and native cattle and declared himself the Orient's all-around champion of 1942.

Rodeo began after the long cattle drives of the mid-1800s when cowboys gathered informally to let off steam competing against each other in the everyday skills of the cowhand—roping, riding, tangling with bucking horses and wild bulls.

Over the years rules and equipment were standardized, judging streamlined, prize money increased, and the freewheeling entertainment of the 1800s evolved into the modern sport of professional rodeo.

In 1979, the Prorodeo museum was opened in Colorado Springs. It captures the flavor and history of rodeo as well as honoring the cowboys, past and present, who created it.

Here the visitor can learn the fine points of saddle bronc riding, how to judge a rider's performance and get the jolting sensation through film with stereo sound what it's like to ride a bucking Brahma bull. Other films trace the historic development of rodeo.

The Prorodeo Hall of Champions is located just north of Colorado Springs on I-25 at Exit 147. Hours are 9 a.m.–5 p.m. daily, Memorial Day through Labor Day. Winter hours are 9 a.m.–4:30 p.m. Tuesday through Saturday; noon–4:30 p.m. Sundays; and closed Mondays. Admission is charged to help defray expenses of the nonprofit museum. Call (303) 593-8847.

COURTESY OF U.S. DEPARTMENT OF THE INTERIOR

Garden of the Gods hiking

Garden of the Gods

The wonders of nature blend together at the **Garden of the Gods** to create one of the most varied natural settings in Colorado. Established as a free city park in 1909, the almost 1,000 acres are filled with silent and unyielding red sandstone rock formations, including Gateway Rocks, Cathedral Spires and the Balanced Rock. Grasslands meet mountain forests to provide contrasts of scenic beauty.

A common resident of the park is the great horned owl, whose keen light-gathering eyes and superior hearing make it an effective nighttime hunter.

Hike, picnic and horseback ride to fully appreciate the park's natural beauty. But most of all, bring your camera and photograph these wonders (especially at sunset or sunrise when the low sun accents the naturally colorful redstone).

Open daily 8:30 a.m.–5 p.m., off U.S. 24, Colorado Springs.

The Broadmoor

The **Broadmoor** is the only major Colorado resort that has 14,110-foot Pikes Peak for a backdrop, and it is the state's only hotel that has been awarded Mobil's coveted Five Stars for more than 25 years in a row.

Luxury and elegance, charm and convenience, taste and class seem happily combined here in the most scenic setting six miles southwest of Colorado Springs. And where else would you find a resort with its own zoo, its year-round skating rink, three golf courses and eight restaurants?

The Broadmoor's accommodations remain pure Grand Hotel. The sports facilities—spread over 5,000 acres—are like a country club's, and the personnel make up a mini-United Nations. The chefs are French, Swiss, German. The waiters are often South American. When the Russian ice hockey teams come to play at Broadmoor's **World Arena**, one of the resort's staff members does the interpreting. Even off-season, the **International Center**, a 2,400-seat auditorium, provides famous entertainers and shows from around the world. The resort's public rooms remain superposh: original Toulouse Lautrecs, authentic 400-year-old Chinese antiques, marble especially quarried in Italy, Puerto Rican carpets. True to form, even the bedspreads were imported from Spain.

Through the years, the Broadmoor acquired a fleet of 72 Cadillacs for Pikes Peak excursions. The zoo has rare animals from Sumatra to Siberia. The Broadmoor's cog railway takes guests up Cheyenne Mountain. There are the spa's enormous greenhouses, a ski slope with chairlifts, a cinema, 16 tennis courts and a glassed-in swimming pool. Browsers will find shops of all kinds. In Broadmoor's bars and bistros, liquor flows like the Colorado afternoon rain. But to some visitors, the most enthralling part is the food.

The resort's eight dining areas excel in variety. Take breakfast, for example. Forty choices, reminiscent of the first class on a transatlantic ship. Lunches can be taken among exotic flowers and palms. (A behind-the-scenes aside: one man has no other task but to bake the daily consumption of French bread.) At night, the Broadmoor's own ice carver goes into action. A simple dinner? Ask for the **Golden Bee** location; it has a succulent steak and kidney pie. (The pub was imported from England, stick by stick.)

For fancier fare, try the **Charles Court Restaurant** or the Louis XV-style **Penrose Room** where you dance to valse music after the Romanoff caviar, the Foie Gras de Strasbourg, the roast pheasant, rack of lamb, duck Bigarde or the four veal

Broadmoor Resort, Colorado Springs

Lovely, luxurious Broadmoor Resort, Colorado Springs, is busy in winter, too

dishes. (Consternation reigned some years ago when King Hussein ordered a hot dog; the chef was prepared for quails in nests of artichoke bottoms with chestnut puree.)

On a typical evening, the Penrose Room sees the like of their Royal Highnesses, the Grand Duke and Grand Duchess of Luxembourg, a Colorado governor and other notables. Planned and supervised by Austrian-trained Food and Beverage Director Siegfried Faller and longtime European Maitre D' Hotel Helmut Meyer, the menu is kept simple:

Potage Talleyrand
Paupiettes of Dover Sole
Vin Blanc Fleurons
* * *

Sorbet Au Fine Champagne
* * *

Filet of Beef Wellington
Truffle Sauce
Bouquetiere of Fresh Vegetables
* * *

Kentucky Bibb Lettuce
* * *

Strawberries Flambe
Petite Fours Glace
* * *

Demitasse
* * *

Liqueurs
* * *

Wines

Chateau St. Jean Chardonnay
Silver Oak Cabernet Sauvignon
Domaine Chandon, Nappa Valley

Such meals can be worked off with "strenuous" Broadmoor sports like shuffleboard, trap and skeet shooting, walks around the lake or riding the electric golf carts on three 18-hole courses. ("The caddies do everything but hit the ball," confides one pro.) More adventurous *sportifs* can rent water skis, canoes, rowboats, paddleboats, horses, bicycles, tandems (for honeymooners), or skates. You can share the indoor ice rink with professionals,

One of the Broadmoor's three golf courses & golf club

Broadmoor Resort/Colorado Springs

who train here for TV spectaculars and films. You can also bowl, hunt, fish, dance or climb peaks.

The Broadmoor Resort actually began in the 1850s with a Silesian count. He hoped to create another Monte Carlo against the backdrop of Colorado's mountainscape. Eventually, two Philadelphians, Charles Tutt and Spencer Penrose, took over. They'd gotten rich in Cripple Creek mining and real estate; as world travelers, they knew what they wanted: a regal Renaissance-style hotel.

The Broadmoor's doors opened on June 29, 1918; among several notables, the first to register was John D. Rockefeller, Jr. Since that day there has been a stream of industrialists, diplomats, movie moguls, film stars, plus titled ladies and gentlemen. They mingle nicely nowadays with anyone who can afford this pricey year-round retreat. (An hour's tennis costs as much as a meal at an average New York restaurant.)

Part of the year is superbly organized convention time for

the world's cardiac surgeons, trial judges, diamond dealers or the Inner Executive Circle of Germany's Mercedes-Benz Company.

Excellence doesn't have to clash with size: The Broadmoor offers some 100,000 square feet of meeting space, enough chairs and other furniture for a gathering of 2,400 people and well-appointed rooms for 2,100 guests. Among them are celebrities galore. Be prepared to dress accordingly.

The (deluxe) Broadmoor isn't for economy travelers; bring lots of travelers checks or your best credit card—Diner's, Visa, or MasterCard are not acceptable. For more information: The Broadmoor, P.O. Box 1439, Colorado Springs, CO 80901; (303) 634-7711. In Colorado, call 623-5197.

Pikes Peak Cog Railway

The year was 1806; the discoverer of Colorado Springs's "Great Mountain" was Lt. Zebulon Montgomery Pike. Neither he nor any of his party got even close to the summit due to bad weather and perhaps a lack of planning. At that time it certainly wasn't conceivable that one of America's most unusual railroads ever constructed would carry thousands of persons to its summit.

Today no visit to Colorado Springs would be complete without a trip on the country's highest railroad to the summit of famous Pikes Peak. The **Pikes Peak Cog Railway**, which is 46,158 feet long, climbs from an elevation of 6,571 feet at the Manitou Springs station, to 14,110 feet at the summit. This is a vertical gain of 7,539 feet or an average of 846 feet per mile. Actually, the distance is longer than any covered by the famous cog wheel rails in Switzerland.

Along the entire route, you'll be treated to a continuous panorama of scenery. At the 11,578 foot level, the trains emerge from a sea of quaking aspen into the windswept stretches of timberline and climb into the Saddle where you get an unparalleled view of Manitou Springs and of Garden of the Gods in the valley below. You also see the vast expanses of the Great Plains stretch indefinitely.

On clear days it is possible to spot Denver 75 miles to the north of Colorado Springs and the Sangre de Cristo Mountains in Southern Colorado. The view of the west is astounding; on the horizon mile upon mile of snowcapped giants rise into the blue Colorado sky. As the Swiss-made train reaches the summit

Pikes Peak scenery enhanced by Broadmoor Resort

of Pikes Peak, you can walk up heights to an observation tower on top of the old Summit House, which contains a curio shop, information desk and a concession counter for light lunches. (Or bring your own brown bag.)

You reach Manitou Springs from Colorado Springs via U.S. 24. Continue west on Manitou Avenue, turn left at Ruxton. The depot is at 515 Ruxton.

The Pikes Peak Cog Railway leaves Manitou Springs at 9 a.m. and 2 p.m. daily May–October. Extra trains in July and August. Round trip is 3 hours, 10 minutes. For reservations, call (303) 685-5401 in Manitou Springs.

Royal Gorge

Royal Gorge! The 1,200-foot-deep canyon fetches over 500,000 sightseers a year. Travelers plumb the rocky canyon depths via a steep incline railway, or drive across a mighty suspension bridge—allegedly the world's highest—or see it all from the bottom as railroad passengers.

There is also the tram.

Like similar ones in Stateline, California and Sandia Peak, New Mexico, the Royal Gorge cabin is painted a fire-red. It takes 35 passengers. A guide-conductor will assure any timid riders that the tram will not fall into the Arkansas River, which runs way below. "We have three braking systems," the conductor will say. "And an extra motor, just in case." In the terminals, about 100 tons of concrete and steel anchor the big cables for the conveyance.

It took a helicopter to string the pilot cable. It also took $350,000 of good Texas money to rig up the Colorado tourist attraction.

All of this adds up to a clever accumulation of conversation pieces for out-of-state visitors. First of all, you have the canyon itself. It has been compared to the Grand Canyon. The colors are reds, mauves, yellows, browns. The chasm is so deep that it stopped Lt. Zebulon Pike in 1806. He just couldn't make it across. (Pikes Peak was named after him, although he didn't scale that one either.) By 1878, after a lot of fighting between two railroads, engineers had built their tracks along the river. Then in 1929, ladies in long fur coats and their escorts in ancient automobiles drove up to see the sensation of the year, the Royal Gorge Bridge. It's still there, five decades later.

You can drive across the wooden planks, or even hike over to the other side. In addition, you can step into one of the

Royal Gorge, Colorado

112

Incline Railway cars, and slowly rumble down to the Arkansas River. The five-minute ride is deafening because you always have many excited children aboard.

The Incline conveyance dates back to the early thirties. During the sixties, the promoters bought an additional family satisfier. This is a little scale model train, a replica of an 1863 Southern Pacific. The train chugs around the Royal Gorge Park. Along the way, you may see deer, trees, cacti, bushes and miles of granite. Royal Gorge also contains various nature trails. Films are sold at the visitor's center, from where you can send postcards with the "Royal Gorge, Colorado" postmark. Other people like to send home a picture of Point Sublime, depicting many caves, craters and rock slabs.

The myriad amusements are open all year. The charges for the various modes of transportation are reasonable. Or you can try it all without paying. Just bring a long rock climbing rope, a solid pair of boots, and enough expertise to get down a perpendicular 1,200-foot rock.

The Royal Gorge is located eight miles west of Canon City via U.S. 50. Canon City is southwest of Colorado Springs and west of Pueblo. Royal Gorge Scenic Railway, Canon City, CO 81212; (303) 275-5485.

Devil's Head Trail

The **Devil's Head Trail,** in the Ramparts Range west of the little community of Sedalia (south of Denver) is one of the state's most scenic mountain trails. It got its name from the red rock formation that sticks out like two horns. You walk up through deep pine forests interspersed with aspen, past giant red cliffs. The trail's length—just 1-3/8 miles—doesn't sound like much; it climbs steeply, though, and includes a 1,000 foot vertical elevation gain. (The summit is at 9,747 feet, the parking lot at 8,800 feet.)

Along the way you get views of the fourteeners (peaks over 14,000 feet high) and the Great Plains. Benches line the uphill paths for the tired. Motorized vehicles (including trail bikes) are outlawed in the ascent to Devil's Head.

Driving directions? From Denver, take Santa Fe (U.S. 85) south to Sedalia (13 miles); turn west toward Deckers (SR 67) and make another left turn onto the Rampart Range Road (Co. Rd. 5) until you see the Devil's Head sign.

Joy cometh from hiking!

Camp Hale

Camp Hale was nicknamed "Camp Hell" by the Mountain Troopers, who first trained here, 18 miles north of Leadville. From 1942 to 1945 the camp served the famous World War II Tenth Mountain Division. Much of their tough battle preparations took place at the chilly 9,500 feet above sea level, on 6,500 mountain acres, surrounded by 12,000-foot snow giants.

The altitude and the thin air took their toll on young recruits from the Midwest; the new arrivals couldn't sleep at first and felt weak during the day. Smoke from 300 barrack chimneys and railroads hung over the camp, and you could hear a lot of coughing.

Camp Hale days often started at 4:30 a.m. with 15-mile marches through blizzards. Packs weighed 80 pounds or more, and the troopers would be pulled backward. The army skis were often so stiff that they sank into the snow. Some southern and midwestern fellows, recruited at the last minute, termed skis their "torture boards." Each time a novice lifted a leg, his muscles hurt. The arms ached, too, from the unaccustomed efforts. The Camp Hale-based mountain warfare soldiers were made to climb 12,000-foot peaks on skis while the temperature could fall to 20 degrees below zero.

To get these men ready for combat against German *Gebirgsjäger* troops, the U.S. Army made even the basic training as realistic as possible. For a Camp Hale "Infiltration Course," the troopers had to crawl under barbed wire for an hour. Then, suddenly, machine guns with live shells shot directly over their heads. Fifty-pound charges of dynamite blew up right and left. Occasional mistakes would cause actual injuries.

Life at Camp Hale was never monotonous; the Tenth Mountain Division troops were employed to test Arctic snow vehicles and battle station rescue toboggans. Troopers trained on large snowshoes and learned how to control avalanches. Other men worked with mules and dogs. A Scandinavian explorer was invited to teach the soldiers how to build igloos and other snow caves. Some of the camp's crack skiers and instructors were actually well-known ski racers or ski jumpers like Walter Prager and Torger Tokle; others like Gordon Wren and Steve Knowlton joined U.S. Olympic ski teams after World War II.

The training of these troops turned even tougher in February, 1944, when the Tenth Mountain men were sent on their first

PHOTO BY MCKENNA

The story of the Tenth Mountain Division, which trained near Leadville, Colorado is an important one for the state

"D-series" maneuvers. They climbed Colorado's Tennessee Pass, and moved for 30 days into the icy wilderness. Snows were so deep that supply vehicles couldn't get through. Loads were so heavy (up to 90 lbs.) that only the best troopers could make it. Despite the 35-degree-below temperatures, no fires were allowed. After devouring K-rations, the food ran out. The struggling Tenth ate almost nothing for three days. When they got back to Hale, there were 100 frostbite cases. Nearby hospitals filled with pneumonia victims.

In summer, the soldiers received instruction in advanced rock climbing techniques; they rappeled down the sheer Colorado cliffs and had to walk on suspended cables and rain-wet logs. Mountaineering knowledge would come in handy. In November, 1944, the Division left Camp Hale for Italy, where the troopers distinguished themselves in battling the Germans.

And the Camp in Colorado? For a time, Camp Hale housed German POWs. After the latter went home, the flagpoles, mule barns and other buildings were forgotten. Suddenly in 1947, the Pentagon brass decided to send other young soldiers to try the Colorado snows for size. Like the former Camp Hale occupants, these infantrymen pitted themselves against the winter cold. When the Korean War broke out in 1950, Camp Hale served the Rangers as a special training ground. A few years later, Army helicopters got their battle tests here. By then, ski troopers no longer seemed as necessary as during World War II days, and most of the military skiing moved out of Colorado and north to Alaska. On July 1, 1965, the buglers sounded a last Camp Hale retreat. Afterward, the U.S. Forest Service once more took control of the area.

During the late 1970s the Forest Service invested money and time to build the Camp Hale picnic areas, hiking paths, a wheelchair trail and parking spaces at the one-time training camp. In May, 1980, many former troopers came up for the dedication of the 20-acre Camp Hale Memorial Campground. It is one of the highest such sites in the United States.

Not far away from camp on Tennessee Pass, a 14-ton slab of granite reaches 20 feet into the sky. The stone's Roll of Honor lists the 990 comrades who gave their lives for the division. Each year on Memorial Day, hundreds of extroopers assemble at Tennessee Pass to remember their companions. Later, they get together to talk about the old days, to swap tales, or to present their families to one another.

Camp Hale, now a U.S. Forest Service Campground, is 180 miles west of Denver via I-70 and SR 91.

Cripple Creek

Back in 1891, the **Cripple Creek** gold strike proved to be the last major gold rush in North America. Within a few years, those mines in the mountains west of Colorado Springs yielded almost a billion dollars worth of the valuable mineral. By 1900, Cripple Creek grew to some 50,000 inhabitants. The miners could patronize 73 saloons, 40 grocery stores, 17 churches, 8 newspapers. Every day, a dozen passenger trains steamed into the depot.

Eventually 500 gold mines operated in the area. Some 8,000 men brought on a gambling, carousing, whoring boom.

Cripple Creek! Ironically, the man who discovered the first gold vein sold his claim for $500 and proceeded to drink it all up. Colorado Springs owes part of its existence to the prospectors. In time, celebrities came and went. Adventurer Lowell Thomas was born in nearby Victor, now a near-ghost town. Groucho Marx once drove a grocery wagon in Cripple Creek.

Abandoned mine, Cripple Creek

Jack Dempsey, for a brief bout a miner, trained and boxed in the region. Financier Bernard Baruch worked as a telegrapher here. Teddy Roosevelt, after a Cripple Creek visit, told the world that "the scenery bankrupts the English language." The politicians arrived in droves to see for themselves.

By and by, gold prices dropped. Production began to slip. The miners scattered. By 1920, fewer than 5,000 people lived here.

And today? Cripple Creek, population 80, attracts some 225,000 summer tourists. They come for the narrow gauge train rides. They pan for gold right on Main Street. They attend one of the 12 weekly summer performances of the classic, professional **melodrama** at the Imperial Hotel. Call (303) 471-8878 for information about dates and times, which can change.

The old railroad depot has become the **District Museum**. Three stories are crammed with mementoes of the mining age. Superbly kept up, the museum is well worth a visit. (Hours: daily 10 a.m.–5:30 p.m. Memorial Day through September; weekends for the rest of the year.)

The local folks are calmly friendly despite the tourist hubbub. Cripple Creek jumps with visitors all summer. They flock to the red brick souvenir and antique shops, where a 1929 beer bottle or 1950s glass pitcher sells as if it were a rare treasure. You can watch the donkeys on Bennett Avenue, buy cowboy boots in a real western store, eat home-cooked food in little cafes. Main Street bustles with some shops that sell tacky merchandise from Hong Kong or Taiwan. The cars jostle for a place to park.

Not many travelers venture on foot beyond the central core of this community. Yet visual rewards await those who make the most of Cripple Creek's lovely location. It is nestled among the Colorado hillsides, which climb from town (elevation: a high 9,494 feet) in every direction. Nature awaits the walker who leaves the red brick confines and heads for the slopes of conifers and aspen trees. The mountains here are studded with old mines, which you reach by hiking up the abandoned roads past rusting machinery, past the old wooden mine trestles, past the piles of forgotten ore. The **Mollie Kathleen Gold Mine** still attracts paying visitors who can tour the mine.

Cripple Creek deserves more than a few hasty hours. At least one overnight stay makes sense. Suggestions? If possible, try to get a reservation at the restored Victorian (moderate) **Imperial Hotel**, (303) 689-2713, which usually stays open through early October but closes for the winter. The velvet carpets, the authentic turn-of-the-century furniture and brass beds are all

Cripple Creek, Colorado has some picturesque old houses

in excellent order. The Imperial has a handsome cherrywood bar and a Victorian dining room with good food and courteous service. This 50-room establishment belongs to the prestigious Association of Historic Rocky Mountain Hotels (1-800-626-4886) and the Imperial owners are savvy about the region. They produce and stage the well-known classic melodrama. Cripple Creek's entertainment, lodging and meals are all moderately priced.

Cripple Creek is 45 miles west of Colorado Springs. From here, it can be reached via U.S. 24 west, then SR 67. The Chamber of Commerce address: Box 650, Cripple Creek, CO 80813; (303) 689-2169.

The trip will be a memorable one.

Leadville and the Tabors

This is a story of love and power, of wealth and poverty, of joys and tragedy, of a Colorado mining town whose fortunes flourished and vanished. A story so extraordinary that it became the subject of an opera, a play and many biographies, some of them bad ones.

The characters were bigger than life. Begin with Horace Austin Warner Tabor, a one-time Vermont stonecutter and his straight-laced hard-working wife Augusta. The couple gave up a Kansas homestead to try their luck first in Denver, then under Pikes Peak, then at Oro City. They arrived in **Leadville** with a rickety wagon and an old ox during the 1860s, some years after the first gold had been discovered in California Gulch.

The Tabors established themselves as best as they could—Augusta with a tiny rooming house and a small bakery, Horace with a store and later a part-time job as mayor.

The Tabors' first break came on Apr. 20, 1878. Two destitute miners, new in town, dropped into Horace's shop. Could he help out with some tools and a basket of groceries? The accommodating mayor agreed to help for a third of whatever minerals they might find. A few days later, some hard digging produced a rich silver vein.

The Tabors were launched. By summer, that first mine—the Little Pittsburgh—lavished $8,000 a week on its owners. Before long, there was $100,000 worth of silver per month; this was followed by other Tabor ventures, all successful. In time, he invested in many mines, owned a good chunk of the local bank, built the Leadville Opera House, erected mansions in the mining

119

town and in Denver. He owned a lot of real estate and a hotel. By 1879, Leadville had 17 independent smelters; it took 2,000 lumberjacks to provide enough wood to fire the machinery that processed the silver riches. Thanks to Tabor's new wealth and almost daily discoveries of more ore, the immigrants flooded to Leadville in droves. Celebrities like the "Unsinkable" Molly Brown showed up as did various Dows, Guggenheims and Boettchers.

Marshall Sprague, a western mining authority, describes in *Money Mountain* the hustle and bustle when thousands streamed across the Continental Divide to Leadville. The road was "jammed with wagons, stages, buggies, carts. There were men pushing wheelbarrows, men riding animals, men and dogs driving herds of cattle, sheep, pigs and goats."

Tabor soon bought an additional mine—the Matchless. He prospered while Leadville grew to a city of 30,000. Oscar Wilde appeared in Tabor's famous Opera House. The Chicago Symphony Orchestra and the Metropolitan Opera came there, to faraway Colorado. Well-known singers, ballet dancers, actresses and entertainers arrived to perform.

H. A. W. Tabor became a millionaire many times over. He was a tall man, moustached, kindly, and, as a local historian writes, "outgoing, gregarious, and honest as the falling rain." By contrast, Horace was married to an unloving woman who although she worked hard, brought Tabor no happiness. She nagged; she was prim and humorless. Colorado's richest man thought he deserved better.

Horace Tabor's luck changed one day in 1882. That evening, the 50-year-old silver magnate saw Elisabeth Doe-McCourt in the restaurant of Leadville's Clarendon Hotel.

"Baby" Doe was 22—a beauty with shining blue eyes and curly dark blonde hair. Round-faced and charming, she'd been born into an Irish immigrant family of 14 children. Baby Doe had just emerged from a brief, unhappy marriage with an unsupportive miner in Central City. Recently divorced, she had the good sense to look for a better partner in booming Leadville. She was a respectable young woman. And her search was crowned by success.

What began as a simple flirtation deepened into an abiding love that scandalized the Rockies and became the celebrated story of Colorado's opera, the *Ballad of Baby Doe* by Broadway veterans John Latouche and Douglas Moore.

Horace and Baby Doe were snubbed by Denver High Society when Tabor divorced his cold wife Augusta, who allegedly received a $500,000 settlement. H. A. W. soon married his new love. The wedding took place in Washington, D.C., in the presence of President Chester Arthur and other dignitaries. Baby Doe received a $90,000 diamond necklace and she wore a $7,500 gown.

Although young, she actually had greater substance than most of her biographers gave her credit for. She was honest and loyal, helpful to others and interested in a variety of things. Best of all, she was in love with her much older Colorado husband. Her love was returned.

The Tabors lived the lavish life of luxury to the hilt. Most historians estimate that the Tabors spent some $100 million. Horace Tabor made few worthwhile investments. For a brief time, he was elected to the U.S. Senate.

In 1893, disaster struck Leadville. Silver was replaced by paper money. The nation experienced a financial panic.

The Tabors were ruined. The mines began to fail. Real estate was sold to satisfy creditors.

The couple moved to Denver, still deeply in love. Thanks to some contacts, Horace got a postmaster's job for a short time. But the financial plunge must have been too much for him. Soon he was ailing. His final hours came on Apr. 10, 1899, at Denver's Windsor Hotel. His wife Baby Doe was by his side, holding his hand.

Before Horace Tabor died, he once more spoke about his Matchless Mine in Leadville. It had long played out after yielding some $1 million during its 14 years of operation. "Hold on to the Matchless," Tabor whispered. "It'll make millions again."

Baby Doe kept her promise. She moved back to Leadville. Penniless, she lived in a shack beside the mine pit for 36 years. She remained faithful to Tabor.

During the winter of 1935, while in her seventies, she shopped at a local grocery for some food. The grocer gave her a ride home in his truck. She was dressed in tatters. Her feet were sheathed in sack cloth instead of shoes. The cabin next to the Matchless Mine was squalid but she kept a rifle in it, protecting her mine.

Leadville's altitude is more than 10,000 feet. It gets cold there on winter nights. Baby Doe Tabor was found in her shack on

Mar. 7, 1935. She had frozen to death. No one knows how long the body had been there. Ironically, there were some unopened boxes with new blankets sent by some Leadville sympathizers, which the dying woman had refused to use. Pride.

The Tabors are buried side by side in Denver. The *Ballad of Baby Doe* was added to the New York City Opera's repertoire shortly after its 1956 debut in Central City, Colorado. The role of Baby Doe was among the first that the then newcomer Beverly Sills sang for a company she now heads.

And how about the current Leadville? The city has seen three decades of modest restoration, and you notice many red brick buildings on main street. Tabor's **Opera House** still stands. The tiny **Matchless Mine cabin** has become a mini-museum. The original **H. A. W. Tabor home**, where he lived with Augusta, can be visited by tourists. Unfortunately, the Leadville city fathers do not support interest in history during the winter months.

The Tabor sites are closed from Labor Day to Memorial Day. Leadville can be reached fom Denver by I-70 and the Copper Mountain turnoff. For more information: Leadville–Lake County, Chamber of Commerce, P.O. Box 861, Leadville, CO 80461; (303) 486-0418.

Colorado Autumn

"The forests are shouting with color," John Steinbeck once wrote.

It's the sudden September frost that produces the spectacle that exalts Coloradans, brings them out of their homes and offices, autumn after autumn. Look into the local newspapers; follow the color photographers, the Sunday painters, the young couples. Exodus to the Rockies! See the aspen trees! The leaves suddenly turn on like so many bright lights. They dazzle. They glow among the deep green of the firs. There are entire aspen forests in these mountains.

The largest groves generally are found between elevations of 8,000 to 10,000 feet. Colors start at the higher elevations and spread their way down as the season progresses. A bright golden yellow predominates, with varying shades of brilliant reds, browns and oranges interspersed with the green of the slower changing leaves and the surrounding conifers.

There is a lyrical something about these "quaking" trees when you're alone among them; the golden leaves tremble in the

Aspen trees in autumn at Trout Lake, Sheep Mountain near Telluride

slightest breeze, make gentle sounds of applause, talk to themselves, or send messages to the raspberry bushes. You'll see the gold and copper all over the state from the end of September through early October: in Aspen itself, in Winter Park, along the Ramparts Range Road from Colorado Springs to Sedalia, beside the Peak-to-Peak Highway between Nederland and Allenspark, west of Boulder. "Aren't the aspen beautiful?" people ask, setting out to see them before winter blows down from the Rockies. Of course, it depends on how much time you have. Six hours? A day? Two? Then consider a good circle tour: Denver, Idaho Springs, Silver Plume, Breckenridge, Fairplay, Denver. No toll roads. Easy motoring.

Begin with U.S. 6, the more spectacular because it's carved out of deep canyons, where the upper rocks are highlighted by the sun. Up to the little mountain community of Idaho Springs (altitude 7,540 feet), up to the big highway, with the peaks rising on both sides. The aspen trees shine like so many lamps among the firs and spruces, and after you're through Georgetown (which is worth visiting), you seem to be in the Alps: the mountains go up steeply now, and the valley's narrow. Up, up to the Continental Divide (11,992 feet) and down from the massive Loveland Pass to the Dillon reservoir. The sun skips across these lake waters with their small marina sailboats, fishing boats, canoes! In Frisco, swing left into SR 9, which still circles this handsome reservoir. Grasslands now, gold, brown, green, leading to the pivot of the tour. Breckenridge!

This little mining community is once more on the verge of a bonanza. In 1859, it was gold. Now it's real estate and second homes for airline people, retired corporation presidents, and skiers. Yet, you couldn't tell this boom from the looks and feeling here. Breckenridge remains congenial, unpretentious, informal, western. The children are running across the silent brown pine needles, some teenagers fish for trout in the transparent Blue River.

One of the local cowboys packs families into the back country for a horseback ride or for hunting deer, and another entrepreneur sends jeeps into the wilderness. (The driver acts as a guide.) At the west part of town, though, there is too much civilization in the shape of too many condominiums.

It's peaceful again as you drive through thick forests past beaver ponds to little-known, ever-so-gentle Hoosier Pass. Golden brown-yellow meadows: faded green lichened rocks, and hardly a house in sight. Impressive 14,000-foot peaks all around: Quandary Peak, Mt. Lincoln, Mount Sherman. Placer Valley, where the aspen trees brighten the pine woods. With a population of 500, Fairplay is the "big" town now, but you're through quickly. Suddenly, clouds in this bright-blue sky; a quick autumn rain. The horses and cows and sheep stand in these darkening fields patiently while the water comes down. Half an hour later, along the South Platte River, the sun bursts through the trees again. At Grant, U.S. 285 narrows and curves along the river past nice campsites that should be full but aren't. (Few tourists after Labor Day.) All the way to Denver, the names spell nature, forest, Colorado.

Pine Junction. Deer Creek. Conifer. Indian Hills.

A few last golden aspen trees followed by russets and reds of maples and oaks. Then Morrison, where the orchards are thick with purple apples. At the lower altitude, and out of the mountains, the air warms you once more. Pleasant autumn. After some 175 miles, the Colorado circle tour ends where it began. But what a six-hour world between!

From U.S. 6, west of Denver, follow I-70 to Frisco, SR 9 to

Breckenridge, from where you return to Denver via U.S. 285.

The Cowboy Still Rides

The chute opens and Joe Alexander, champion bareback rider, holds on to the horse's riggings with one hand. The horse rears wildly, resenting the man, hooves in all directions, a bucking, pitching, twisting, snorting wild-eyed rebel. The cowboy's hat flies high, landing in the dust.

He has been on the horse for five seconds now, and he still hangs on. He leans all the way back, ankles still spurring, his shoulder blades against the animal's spine. The man's outstretched arm hits the horse's bones. It's a human against beast. Six seconds now. Seven. Eight.

The buzzer sounds. Alexander jumps safely onto the ground.

Eight seconds of bareback riding can seem like eight hours. It still takes a strong, bold person to ride at rodeos.

These Wild West riding competitions are an important income source for some Colorado cowboys. After all, the cattle business in the United States has shrunk during the past decades. Much of the profit has been taken out. These days, ranches are fewer, and, although some of the successful ones are in southern Colorado, they're smaller than they used to be, with only about 300 animals each.

At one time, hundreds of men were needed to drive 6,000 or more Black Angus, Herefords, Shorthorns and other breeds to market. Nowadays, trucks do the job. The oldtime cowhand had to feed the stock in winter—a job often done by helicopters these days.

In sheer numbers, the Western cowboy has diminished but a few large Colorado ranches still need these rugged, underpaid men to brand cattle in spring, to put up and repair fences, to rope the creatures, and to look after their health. One ranch manager, for a big cattle company 30 minutes south of Denver, still rounds up his stock twice a year. In the saddle for long hours, he enjoys the freedom of his 10,000 acres. He dresses the part, too. Cowboy hat, leather vest, leather belts with elaborate buckles, levis, buckaroo boots. He says he enjoys the heat and getting dirty; few people know that he has a law degree.

Many cowboys have learned some of the veterinary skills; they know a lot about the pharmaceuticals and the vaccinations of the present-day Western cattle industry. Likewise, cowboys learn about feeding and they help with cattle sales. A few hardy cowpunchers still ride with their herds from mountain pasture to pasture, all summer long. The riders certainly must look after their horses. And Colorado is the state where it all happens.

This leads back to the rodeo circuit, which has become lucrative for some Colorado cowboys of all ages who can travel to some of more than one thousand competitions that go on during the year in North America. In addition, there are hundreds of nonsanctioned amateur and intercollegiate rodeos and even some for kids.

Some 30 million American tourists travel to the big spectacles. For ten days each July, for instance, some of the Colorado-based cowboys and cattle flock to Calgary, in Canada's province of Alberta, where the purses keep increasing. Altogether, some $5 million in prizes go to riders in the United States and Canada; at Wyoming's famous Frontier Days alone, $600,000 in rodeo winnings are split by a cast of 1,500.

The top cowboys often own sizable cattle ranches themselves. The famous ones sometimes fly their own planes.

Rodeo actually began as an exciting pastime of those rough, tough cowhands who rode the range and drove the herds of beef to market. "Ride 'em cowboy" was not much more than a contest of bravery among cowboys of the Old West. From these unassuming beginnings, rodeo has evolved into a Big Business.

Some Colorado cowboys (and cowgirls) take care of the horses at dozens of the state's dude ranches. The latter are basically rustic, with Western-style furniture against a log cabin backdrop. The rooms often contain fur-covered sofas, rugged granite fireplaces, elk antlers on the walls, or framed words of cowboy wisdom. The cooking is plain, the food plentiful and included for the help and customer alike. There is a warm feeling about these enclaves, nestling deeply in Colorado's forests, straddling mountaintops, overlooking rivers that rush and splash. The lodges are usually built of the pine or spruce woods and the stone rock of the region. The windows will surely look out upon pretty scenes.

The cowboys at these ranches often prepare breakfast for the guests on a hillside. At one well-known vacation center, the head wrangler teaches riding to first-timers and gives equestrian advice to others. Cowboys usually lead the various outings.

Meet Leslie (Les), a typical Colorado cowboy who owns one characteristic dude ranch west of Denver. Les employs a cook who feeds the guests, a clerk who checks them in, a lodge manager who looks after details. Les himself is mostly involved with the horses. His life always evolved around animals.

He hates to wear suits, and he hates to go to the city (where he keeps an apartment all the same). He doesn't like fancy talk, or talk, period. He likes horses and dogs better than people, yet at this moment, he leads a group of people—experienced riders all—on another daily excursion, his second one today. He is not outgoing, yet he coddles and protects his "dudes," and no lives were ever lost out here.

Les loves horses more than anything. At dawn Les had walked over to the red barn and the corral. He'd whistled. His mare, Frosty, came right out. Animal and man were one as Les rode up with the early risers, some of them very slow, typical tourists, at first fearful and uncertain. As always, two other helpers galloped ahead of the group to fry the eggs and get the pancakes ready on the griddle. The coffee boils and sends up whiffs of flavor.

Many cowhands know how to shoe horses, know how to treat the sick ones and please the rest.

Les is so much around the hoofed creatures that he has been stepped on, backed into and severely kicked by horses. One time, three of his ribs were broken by one of his animals. Les spent a week in the hospital, cursing and cussing. Yet he wouldn't give it all up for anything. His nostrils love the sweet smell of hay and manure, and his ears like to pick up the comforting, caressing sound of horses feeding.

Some cowboys certainly show an adaptable spirit. A few of them, for instance, also take their guests hunting for wild game in the higher mountain ranges. At one horse center, Colorado's famous luxurious C Lazy U Ranch, two of the cowboys adjusted to the times and to fads: they learned to cross-country ski and now take the guests on ski trips in winter.

Some wranglers don't work at these ranches; they're independent and merely operate their own stables on a busy highway, looking for other work in winter.

Inspired by Western cowpokes, a whole industry has sprung up in the United States. Much of the fashion in jeans, denim jackets and cowboy boots harks back to the Old West. (At the dude ranches, meanwhile, the city dwellers arrive garbed in Western wear with large Western hats.)

Colorado's "cowboy artists," while no longer on horseback or herding cattle, drive jeeps into the wilderness with their easels and oil paints. Art galleries in Denver sell the artists' output—sceneries with wild buffalo and paintings of wild horses, high mountains and western prairies.

Colorado's cowboys are featured in American filter cigarette ads. And cowboys even brought on a special kind of country music, which is now especially popular in America's South. Several museums around the United States exhibit cowboy gear, including saddles and spurs, as if these items were rare treasures.

Cowboy poets enjoy popularity, too. Their output can be read in newspapers; national magazines publish their verse and even book publishers collect them. Poems hang framed on dude ranch walls. The message can be brief and wise, as this little item from an anonymous author: "Never was there a cowboy who couldn't be throwed, never a bronc who couldn't be rode."

Most of the rhymes are simple, basic, perhaps a little primitive. Example? At one Western ranch, a wrangler dug deeply to express the horsey west in a poem:

> May Your Horse Never Stumble
> May Your Cinch Never Break
> May Your Belly Never Grumble
> May Your Heart Never Ache.

The poem speaks a universal language.

Still a special person, the Colorado cowboy rides on.

Great Sand Dunes National Monument

Sand dunes in Colorado? What a surprise! Geologists say that the sand stretches such as those of the **Great Sand Dunes National Monument** are usually the handiwork of the world's oceans. Didn't the salt water have millions of years to crush, mash and pulverize the land? The sea pushed, licked and retreated, eroding rocks into small particles and grinding earth to fine silt. Moreover, winds blew sand grains from the mountains to our plains. Erosive forces and more winds helped fashion sand peaks that crest to 600 feet above the valley floor.

The Great Sand Dunes National Monument looks as if it had been lifted from Africa's Kalahari Desert. White man didn't discover these dunes until 1599 when the Spanish explorers crossed the sands.

According to Colorado historian Richard Grant, pictures taken in 1927 show that the main dunes have undergone very little change in the past 50 years. Except that in 1932 they became a national monument—the Great Sand Dunes.

Great Sand Dunes National Park. "Sunflowers grow among the nations highest dunes."

The monument takes in about 46,000 acres of this ocean of sand. Although there are many activities available, hiking on the dunes is everyone's first choice. Visitors can go anywhere they want. It's best to take off your shoes and wade across the soft water-cooled sand creek, but be sure to wear shoes into the dunes. In midsummer the sand can get as hot as 140 degrees.

On the other side of the stream the dunes are incredibly massive—some rising 70 stories above the valley floor—and, due to shadows, deceptively steep. The valley floor is 7,500 feet above sea level, making breathing difficult at first for those not adjusted to the altitude.

But there are few experiences that can compare with being on the dunes. It is like riding in the frozen waves of a storm-blown sea. You climb to the top of a ridge, taking in a view of the gold and tan waves stretching for miles to the towering blue mountains, then descend the trough until you are in a valley completely surrounded by immense hills of sand. The highest dune is located opposite the visitors center, and it takes about three hours to hike to the top and return. From the top you can see nearly the entire area as well as a large segment of Colorado's Sangre de Cristo Range.

Great Sand Dunes National Monument is located on SR 17 in the south central part of the state, just a few miles off U.S. 160, the main east-west highway through southern Colorado. SR 17 is a scenic north-south alternative route to I-25.

Tamarron Resort

Dramatic triangular rocks on one side; wooded mountains on the other. In between, an undulating 18-hole golf course, where elk congregate at dawn under ponderosa pine. Town-houses and a stately, perfectly blending lodge on a 200-foot cliff.

There is room for 850 people here, yet the year-round (deluxe) **Tamarron Resort** remains a secret even to many Denverites. This remote paradise has everything—nature, atmosphere, amenities. The charming, friendly town of Durango is just 18 miles to the south. To the north of Tamarron, you see Colorado's most magnificent Alpine scenery and such legendary communities as Ouray and Silverton. Not far from the five-star resort, the **Mesa Verde National Park** awaits the visitor.

Built at $50 million, Tamarron was always a special oasis for the discriminating traveler. You might call it a little remote. But self-sufficiency and beauty make up or it. You would not easily forget the high-beamed rustic main lodge plus the secluded, elegant condos that nest among hillocks and forests of aspen and fir. (The average altitude: 7,300 feet.) As you begin to size up the 620-acre grounds, you soon realize that for once, you're truly away from it all, safe and secure. The air is pure, the all-season sports on the quiet side. You can take indoor tennis lessons or cross-country ski lessons. Privacy! Tamarron has its own downhill ski runs, complete with one chairlift plus snowmaking. A nonskiing visitor enjoys the sledding, the sleigh rides, an outing on snowshoes. All comers praise the staffed health club and masseurs.

The complex offers several dining places, fashionable shops, children's areas, Ping-Pong, wonderful jeeping, hiking, archery, volleyball facilities. Tamarron's overall ambiance is utterly relaxed, restful, unhurried and unworried.

The prize-winning resort opened in 1974. The lodge features an unusual swimming pool, where you can swim indoors and outdoors. There's skeet and trap shooting. Horseback expeditions depart each day from the stables, bringing you into the one-million-acre **San Juan National Forest.** Guides who are well versed in the history and ecology of the area accompany the riders through the virgin wilderness.

Tamarron Resort near Durango offers golf

For the adventurous, Tamarron offers a myriad of active outdoor possibilities. For instance, the Sports Desk can arrange a rafting trip. Fishing trips are popular. Durango beckons with a historic narrow-gauge railroad, which winds its way over narrow mountain passes. The resort has its own jeeps for high country tours where you can visit old mines and wander among some 50 species of wildflowers.

Just a few miles southwest of Durango is Mesa Verde National Park. Here, the mesa, a natural tableland, rises 1,500 feet from the valley floor, housing a vast network of well-preserved ancient apartment-style dwellings. The latter were built by the Anasazi, a people who vanished nearly a thousand years ago. Mesa Verde is one of the few areas in this country where relics of their culture can be found. Guided tours throughout the day bring alive the history of this past civilization.

Tamarron itself has many classic features. Rough-hewn beams enhance the architecture. Large, old-fashioned fireplaces make you feel comfortable. Mountain views greet you through the windows of all the restaurants and handsome convention rooms. (In summer, top executives of such companies as Quaker

Oats, Polaroid, Aetna and many others meet here.) The staff of 400 is courteous.

Bill Sageser, longtime manager of the luxury retreat, sums it up this way: "We want guests to have a pleasant experience. We want them to have fond memories."

Tamarron, the remote one, certainly succeeds. The beauty of the Colorado setting does its share, of course.

Tamarron is located 18 miles north of Durango. Fly to Durango from Denver and Albuquerque. Or drive via U.S. 550 and the Navajo Trail, U.S. 160. Write Tamarron Resort, P.O. Box 3131, Durango, CO 81302; or phone toll-free 1-800-525-5420 nationwide, 1-800-525-6493 in Colorado, or (303) 247-8801.

Mesa Verde

The admirers of this popular state speak well about Colorado's **Mesa Verde National Park.** It is a ten-hour's drive south of Denver.

Mesa Verde yields an extraordinary educational experience. A very small area here provides you with much that is of

COURTESY OF COLORADO DEPT. OF PUBLIC RELATIONS

Square Tower House, Mesa Verde

archaeological interest. Before you drive the distance, however, you should keep in mind that Mesa Verde differs substantially from other parks. There is no fishing here, nor boating, swimming or rock climbing. Your pets have to be on a leash. And you can see the historic, wondrous Cliff Dwellings only in the company of park rangers.

The 21-mile road from the park entrance curves and swings and rotates upward; its width doesn't approximate that of an interestate highway. You may have trouble if you come in a truck or try to pull a large camper. If you want to stay in the park itself, you can write to the **Far View Motor Lodge** (Mesa Verde, CO 81328). Rooms at the peak of the season are sold out far in advance; the lodge is closed from October 16 to May 14.

A visit to Mesa Verde National Park should therefore be planned with care. Earmark one or two days for the park itself and try to arrive early in the day or during the off season. The historical scene and the colors come through especially well if you can visit Mesa Verde at dawn. The moment you see the sudden, flat-topped plateau, the cliff dwellings of a prehistoric civilization, you'll be happy that you braved the distance. No other national park can equal this one.

Begin with a visit to the park museum for clues to the mysterious Basket Weavers. These Indians left behind an amazing array of agricultural tools, pottery and baskets. The tribes arrived in the area around 450 A.D. and abandoned the site in 1276. It took another 500 years for Spanish explorers to discover the old, russet blocks of stone, the turrets and primitive apartments known as cliff dwellings hanging under a canopy of glorious rock. You will never forget the Balcony House and Cliff Palace.

At its height, the Mesa Verde Plateau supported 50,000 Indians. By the close of the thirteenth century, it was completely deserted. What happened to the Anasazi is not known, but archeologists theorize that a 30-year drought starting in 1276 combined with soil that had been depleted by constant use caused successive crop failures, and the Indians moved further south into New Mexico and Arizona.

The National Park Service does a good job of looking after Mesa Verde's 80-mile area of ponderosa pines, spruce trees, juniper, all laced by a few paths. Not a billboard or soft drink sign in sight.

Balcony House, Mesa Verde National Park

When visiting Mesa Verde you're not too far from the borders of Utah, New Mexico and Arizona. This is butte country. The sky is even bluer here in the southwest. The pleasant summer warmth allows you to dress any way you wish. The plains seem to stretch wider than in the northern state corners. The Colorado peaks resemble those of the Alps, with jutting slopes and deeply carved valleys. (Bring a warm change of clothes.) The people are easygoing and glad to see you come.

After the Mesa Verde experience, your own state or province will never be the same again.

The park entrance is midway between Cortez and Mancos on U.S. 160. It is 21 miles up the side of the mesa to park headquarters.

The Ute Indians

The **Ute Indians** are the oldest continuous residents of Colorado of the seven original tribes who still live in the southwestern part of the state today. For those with an adventuresome Indian spirit, the city of Durango is the gateway to both the **Southern Ute** and **Mountain Ute reservations.**

Nearly a century ago, the Indians accepted government allotments and settled on a strip of land along the Colorado–

New Mexico border, near the present town of Ignacio (population 667). Eventually these Utes became known as the Southern Ute Indian tribe. Claiming over 1,000 members, their headquarters remains in Ignacio today.

Here they have built an Indian Country vacation complex, complete with a 38-room motel, indoor/outdoor pool, museum and a fine arts and crafts shop. The tribe lives on a reservation.

The present-day Ute Indians can hardly be distinguished from any other Americans. Sounds of their TVs, radios and VCRs fill their modern day urban homes. Basketball and swimming are popular reservation sports. Many Indians drive to the nearest towns for shopping, movies and restaurants.

Luckily, their society does allow the dynamic combination of both traditional and modern cultures. Depending upon age, education, job and values, some Indians continue to speak the Ute language. They handmake their clothes and do traditional work in arts and crafts. Other Indians prefer to live the modern American life. The tribe itself and the Bureau of Indian Affairs employ most of the Ute Indians today.

The ancestral home of these native Americans spanned most of the present state of Colorado. Although reigning over a large empire, they lacked a common Ute political organization. Instead, they formed independent bands, which followed their own chiefs. The most famous groups included the Uncompahgre or Tabeguache whose central home was the area around the present sites of Gunnison and Montrose, Colorado; the White River and Yampa bands of northwestern Colorado; the Mouache who roamed along the front range of the Rockies in Colorado; the Capotes who lived in the San Luis Valley of Colorado; and the Weminuche who lived in the San Juan Basin of southwestern Colorado.

While hunting and roaming their enormous territory, the Utes often fought against other tribes; yet the Indians remained on generally good terms with white men who trapped, traded and prospected for gold on Indian lands.

As Anglo settlers streamed onto Colorado's Eastern Slope, the government, fearing trouble between whites and Utes, tried to persuade the Indians to move to the west of the Continental Divide. Finding it difficult to negotiate with so many chiefs, the government designated an Uncompahgre leader, Ouray—his name meant arrow—as the Ute tribal spokesman. Chief Ouray wanted to preserve his home and Ute territory; he resisted departure from the San Luis Valley and surrounding areas.

Finally, under the treaty of 1868, the Indians agreed to move westward.

Subsequent treaties and promises made and broken resulted in combative Indians. Trouble erupted when Utes attacked and killed United States soldiers in the Meeker and Thornburgh massacres, and they were later driven off their lands.

These days, all is peaceful in Southern Colorado, though, and the Indians welcome tourists.

The Southern Ute Indian Reservation is served by the Southern Ute Agency of the Bureau of Indian Affairs, Ignacio, CO 81137.

The Ute Mountain Ute Reservation is served by the Ute Mountain Ute Agency of the Bureau of Indian Affairs, Towaoc, CO 81334.

Crested Butte

Crested Butte is a sizable, scenic ski center, 30 minutes north of Gunnison, Colorado, too far from the big metropolitan cities to attract crowds. (Denver is 235 miles to the northeast.) One local inhabitant explains Crested Butte this way: "In an age plagued by problems of too many people, too many cars and roads and buildings, this kind of country has a special attraction. It seems to have been made *for* people, not *by* them."

Some of the Crested Butte aficionados speak of a feeling "that borders on reverence, a joy of simply being here." The ski area and the nearby mini-mining town of Crested Butte (two miles away) give off a feeling of relaxation. The atmosphere is pastoral, sometimes even somnolent, informal, tolerant, nature-rooted.

These mountains are some of the state's most beautiful. They combine all the power and grace of the Swiss Alps, and you seem to ski in a never-ending symphony of valleys and meadows, of crests and snow fields. Crested Butte is blessed with nicely separated terrain for experts (only 20 percent of the land), intermediates (55 percent) and beginners (25 percent). Beginners are especially fortunate here.

One of the area's major assets is a gently sloping, broad, chairlift-served run on the lower mountain more than a mile long. It is excellent for novice skiers, who at many areas are confined to short, makeshift slopes with minimal lift facilities. The upper mountain holds myriad pleasures for more advanced skiers. One chairlift, for example, serves slopes with an average grade of 44 percent, which experts find challenging (and will scare the daylights out of average types).

The larger part of Crested Butte is for the intermediate skier. This includes a many-trails complex that taps the open ski terrain of Crested Butte's north-side slopes. Here, the snow comes earlier, stays longer and is deeper and lighter than anywhere on the mountain, with an average 33 percent grade, 1,350 vertical feet. Ideal for intermediate skiing, the Paradise Bowl reminds one of Vail's bowls and provides great joys to most visitors.

Crested Butte's lift situation is good, too, thanks to a dozen chairlifts.

The ski school has an important and reliable cross-country program for which the surrounding country seems perfectly suited.

Colorado's choicest cross-country adventure—indeed, a special *piece de resistance* for experts—ties Crested Butte with Aspen, just 28 miles away. (Guides furnished.) Rentals are available in town and at the base lodge shop.

Some of the area's ski clientele never saw snow before. The ski school is therefore a patient one. The names of some ski runs give a good clue to the customers—Houston Trail, Kansas Trail. Charters regularly fly in from states like Georgia, and you'll find some midwestern family trade. It is intriguing to simply sit in front of the base cafeteria and watch the mix of people, especially on weekends. Crested Butte draws from the local state college then, and you'll see the tanned, casual, enamored youth in full bloom: pink-cheeked young women, fellows in jeans, jeans and more jeans.

The town of Crested Butte gets its character from the old mining days, and the streets are full of young and old men with beards, who all look alike. On weekends, you glimpse sheriffs with badges, and there are some town drunks to be taken care of. Night life is limited to saloons with loud banjos and other instruments, beer drinking and talking to the multitude of ski bums. Many dogs sit in front of the clapboard buildings; dogs of various shapes leap across the pockmarked streets, or show up at the lived-in ski area. Food and lodging prices range from moderate to expensive. Accommodations are available in old lodges and well-worn guests houses, plus condos for the rich. There is also a new hotel.

For more information: Crested Butte is a 30-minute drive north of Gunnison on SR 135. Crested Butte, Mt. Crested Butte, CO 81225; (303) 349-2222.

Denver and the Plains

Denver: A Short History

There were the Spaniards and the Indian tribes—Utes, Cheyennes, Arapahos and Cherokees. Then suddenly came the white prospectors to that prairie wilderness ten miles east of the mountain ramparts. The fate of a tranquil Indian village at the junction of Cherry Creek and South Platte River would be changed forever.

That summer day in 1858, the Anglo visitors found gold in these waters.

Word of the find soon spread. "The New Eldorado!" shouted the midwestern papers. That spring an estimated 150,000 people began the trek across the wide plains aboard wagons and even on foot. Only 40,000 made it or stayed; others turned back.

Gold in paying quantities was far from common. Those first months were very hard. Yet that year, a people's court was organized. The first hotel—The Denver House—opened. Publisher William N. Byers reached Denver on Apr. 21, 1859, with a printing outfit. On April 23 he issued the first newspaper printed in Colorado. William McGaa was the first child born in Denver. Leavenworth and Pikes Peak Express ran the first stage to Denver. The Auraria Post Office was established.

That May, John H. Gregory discovered a vein of goldbearing quartz near what was to become Central City. This was big news and, at first, it nearly evacuated Denver. However, as mines were developed in the mountains, Denver grew in her coming role as an important trade center. Indeed, Horace Greeley suggested, "Go West, young man! Go West, young man!" Denver became the logical jumping off point for the Cripple Creek riches and the huge gold finds of Central City and Black Hawk.

Exaggeratd accounts of the discovery traveled eastward, causing the Gold Rush of 1859. Thousands of fortune hunters hurried across the plains, on foot, on horseback, in wagons, some even pushing handcarts and wheelbarrows. Most of these failed to find the mineral and trudged wearily back home. But they had founded several little habitation clusters variously known as Auraria and Denver City (named after Gen. James W. Denver, territorial governor of Kansas), and these gradually became the capital city of Colorado.

All through the late 1850s and early 1860s, a great mass of people surged back and forth in search of wealth. Conditions were primitive in these Colorado camps. Tents were eventually

Chapter 5
Denver and the Plains

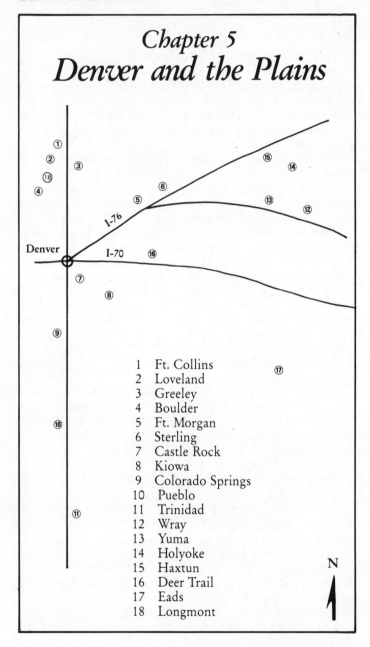

Denver

I-76

I-70

1   Ft. Collins
2   Loveland
3   Greeley
4   Boulder
5   Ft. Morgan
6   Sterling
7   Castle Rock
8   Kiowa
9   Colorado Springs
10   Pueblo
11   Trinidad
12   Wray
13   Yuma
14   Holyoke
15   Haxtun
16   Deer Trail
17   Eads
18   Longmont

N

replaced by huts, which grew into shacks, log cabins and finally houses.

Gold brought more fortune hunters from all over North America, but also Irish engineers, Welsh hard rock miners and other Europeans, 100,000 more people in all. For a period between the 1870s and 1890s, Colorado had so many Germans that the laws were printed in both German and English.

Lots of problems and calamities awaited the city.

Early in 1863, a great fire destroyed much of the business district. The following summer the lush plains were scorched by a drought. The winter was cold beyond all previous experience. Then in the spring of 1864 a flash flood churned along the Cherry Creek sand bed through the city, washing over houses and bridges and killing 20 persons. Nearly one million dollars worth of property was destroyed.

In the wake of these natural disasters, the Indians attacked. Stage stations were sacked, communication and supply lines to the East severed. Denver was left with only weeks' supply of food.

But the city survived, and because of the hardships the local people developed a determination to keep on surviving. When the Union Pacific Railroad bypassed Colorado on its transcontinental route, Denver citizens raised $300,000 and built their *own* railroad to meet the Union Pacific at Cheyenne, Wyoming. Soon the Kansas Pacific crossed the plains. According to historian Richard Grant, "the silver barons built elaborate mansions on Capitol Hill. Gamblers, drifters and gunmen flooded the saloons and gaming halls on Larimer and Market Streets. Bat Masterson tended bar here, Soapy Smith ran the West's largest gang of thieves, crooks and con artists, and anyone who was anyone in the "Old West" paid at least a visit to Denver's mud-filled, honky-tonk streets."

On Aug. 1, 1876, Colorado entered the Union and was called the Centennial State in honor of the 100th anniversary of the Declaration of Independence.

By 1879, The Mile High City had a population of 35,000 and boasted the first telephone service in the West. Soon there was a second boom. One silver mining camp after another suddenly prospered. When the silver played out, Denver settled into a comfortable, respectable life—nearly free of gamblers, drifters and claim jumpers.

Education now became important. In 1887, Gov. Ben H.

The majestic Rockies form an attractive backdrop for Denver's sparkling new skyline.

Eaton told the General Assembly: "The schools of Denver are today equal to the best in the world—equal to those of Boston, Paris or Berlin. The capital of our state is the Athens of the plains, with the glory of ancient Athens."

By 1910 the city had become the commercial and industrial center of the Rocky Mountain region, with a large cattle market and the largest sheep market in the world. Denver was in the process of becoming the nation's second capital, thanks to a proliferation of government offices. This situation is still true today; every second adult seems to work for the federal government, the state or the city.

Many older Denverites still harbor a nostalgic feeling about Colorado Victoriana, and some people are seriously trying to hold on to the city's remaining old mansions. There is public resistance to the wreckers sent by those who prefer the profit of more office buildings and highrise apartment houses. Many of the noted old edifices, the Tabor Theater and the Windsor Hotel among them, had to give way to the modern glass and steel skyscrapers. "Part of Denver died tonight," said a Denverite the day another of the historic hotels was razed. A few of the Victorian homes still exist, complete with the cherrywood dressers and mantelpieces, hat racks and cherrywood mirror frames. The **Brown Palace** and the **Oxford Hotel** still stand.

And while in the city, you may wish to visit some of the old mansions such as the **Molly Brown House**, where history is preserved.

How Denverites Feel About Their City

Even in these transient times, most Denverites refuse to relocate to another city. "Move?" says one executive. "They offered me a promotion on the east coast. But I refused. Stayed on at a lower salary." If you ask longtime Denver people why they're so partial to their city, you'll get a long string of explanations. "We ski. The mountains are close." "We love the many parks and green lawns of the homes." "Do you know a more cosmopolitan place between Los Angeles and Chicago? Denver is *it!*"

The denizens of the Colorado state capital mention the educational and cultural possibilities, the libraries and workshops and seminars, the geographically central location, the generally low unemployment rate, the beautification of the downtown area during the past decade what with **Larimer Square**, the **Tivoli Complex**, the **Westin Center**, the **Sixteenth Street Mall**.

Because the mountains are only 30 minutes away from downtown, Denver attracts a young, energetic population. This dynamic energy is reflected in Denver's nightlife. The city boasts more than 2,000 restaurants, over 100 art galleries, almost 30 theatres, 100 cinemas, an $80 million performing arts center, and dozens of nightclubs, discos, singles bars and concert halls. Denver leads the nation in movie attendance per capita, is in the top five cities for book purchases and is a growing center for jazz. But if there is one thing Denver does well (after 130 years of practice) it is the saloon. The first permanent structure in Denver was a saloon, and today there are sports bars, art bars, fern bars, outdoor cafe bars, English pubs, "Old West" saloons, rock bars, city-overlook bars, Country and Western bars, Art Deco bars, and even bars that don't serve alcohol.

And the legendary climate! Denverites enjoy recreation all year; many outdoor swimming pools are open throughout the four seasons. The Rocky Mountains screen the city from temperature extremes. Spring temperatures are pleasant. When much of the United States swelters in the summer heat, the mountains' air conditioning keeps Denverites cool. It seldom rains. Mean precipitation is only 14 inches annually. Unceasing

Helen Bonfils Theatre Complex at The Denver Center for the Performing Arts

day-after-day torrents are unknown. (Showers last just minutes.) Late autumn—even October and November—can bring exceptionally beautiful weather that the natives call Indian Summer. Winters are mild. The dry mountain air is invigorating, but never extreme. (On occasion, however, temperature inversions and lack of wind make for too much air pollution.)

The climate encourages outdoor pursuits. As a result, Denver has more sporting goods stores and ski shops per capita than any other population center in the world, and a corresponding number of recreation facilities that include free tennis courts, city golf courses and the like.

At the same time, film makers, artists, thinkers all gravitate toward Denver, a city that spent $6 million to build an art museum. The main public library, with its 1,200,000 volumes, happens to be one of the best—and most versatile—in the West. It is at the library desks that you get the feeling of Denver's wide horizons.

Denver's genuine penchant for culture shows up in several ways. On a given evening, the visitor to the state capital could take in a play by Dylan Thomas at the boldly designed **Denver**

Center Theatre. Next door, in the futuristic 2,700-seat **Boettcher Concert Hall,** the music lovers can enjoy the artistry of duo-pianists from Italy, an Israeli violinist, the top singers from the Metropolitan or the Denver Symphony and the 110-member Colorado choir plus soloists excelling in a Händel's *Messiah.* The city has come of age culturally, what with its little theatres, its art cinemas, its ballets and chamber music ensembles. Art galleries beckon by the dozen, and it is not unusual to come upon traveling exhibits from Mexico, Spain, Belgium and other countries.

Local interest is keen in the rest of the world. And Denver's citizens remain helpful and hospitable, especially toward tourists and guests. Just tell a Denverite that you arrived here yesterday from London or Frankfurt or Minneapolis or wherever. Doors will spring wide open. Denverites will show off their clean city; they may want to take you to their homes, where the inevitable sprinklers deepen the green of the lawns and flower gardens.

Denver arouses special interest because of its ethnic variety. The Spanish American population is fascinating for its rich and proud heritage.

In north Denver, you find the classic Italian grocery stores that sell *prosciutto,* salami, black olives and *tonno* as those in Italy. Genuine Italian restaurants serve you homemade pasta and black olives and you drink chianti, just as you would in Naples, Solerno or Parma.

There is a Polish club in Denver, where the young Polish girls still wear the pretty national costumes for their national folk dances.

A small Denver contingent is German-speaking, with a lasting interest in dancing *schuhplattler* and singing all the old songs. The Germans founded an appropriately named Edelweiss Club, a Goethe Club and the *Turnverein,* where the men really do strenuous calisthenics and play soccer on weekends. Denver has its own German *Delikatessen* stores, which import marinated herring from Kiel and Hamburg, Westphalian hams and landjaeger sausages, and sell their customers Nivea suntan creams, German Odol toothpaste and *Der Stern* magazine, much as in Manhattan's Yorkville area.

There is a sizeable Japanese population with its own stores and customs, and a Buddhist Temple for their weddings.

There is also Denver's enthusiasm for international dining.

Well-traveled, polyglot restaurateurs like Pierre Wolfe often appear on TV or radio. Heinz Gerstle, another foreign cuisine expert, has founded a local gourmet club. It should come as no surprise that the city has a number of authentic (and expensive) French eating places (among others, the **Normandy, Quorum, Mont Petit, Le Central**). Denver's dozens of superb oriental restaurants include the well-regarded Mandarin and Szechuan **Golden Dragon** (moderate). The visitor can also dine on genuine Ethiopian, Afghan, Moroccan, Greek, Armenian, Hungarian, Swiss, German, Italian and, of course, on Mexican fare. How about the traveler from the British Isles? On Denver's West side, the **Wuthering Heights** restaurant displays medieval armor and enriches its longish menu with Prime English steak, Filet of Beef Wellington and an English boneless chicken breast (expensive). At the foot of the new downtown skyscrapers, meanwhile, **Duffy's Shamrock Inn** holds court with (inexpensive) Irish home cooking, followed by real Irish coffee. This pub serves a filling supper at a reasonable price.

To be sure, the city's better restaurants, its bistros and more worldly nightspots, its extra elegant central hotels (like the **Westin**) are accustomed to and welcome the visitor from abroad.

Despite the cosmopolitan spirit, Denverites still emphasize the west. You may be taken to lunch at the historic **Buckhorn Exchange** (deluxe); part museum, part restaurant, the Buckhorn serves buffalo burgers and other Wild West fare while stuffed buffaloes, moose and deer stare down from the walls that are also crammed with Old West photos and paintings of Indian chiefs.

You'll hear about the yearly **National Western Stock Show**; here cowboys still buck unbroken horses and wrestle steers. There is cattle auctioning, too. Much Black Angus from Scotland and Herefords that once grazed in Herefordshire.

Usually, Denverites show off the **Museum of Western Art**, or the elegant Western history department of the **Main Library** or the cowboy statues at the **Civic Center**.

You might trust their touristic judgment, what with Denver and environs attracting more than ten million visitors a year. "Smile!" goes one of the state's slogans. "You *live* in Colorado!" And most Denverites smile a lot as they count their blessings.

Denver Metro Convention and Visitors Bureau, 225 W. Colfax, Denver, CO 80202; (303) 892-1112.

Cattle auction

National Western Stock Show

Of all the year-round events that take place in Denver, this one, by golly, is the biggest, longest, most original—a yearly happening that radiates authenticity, excitement, entertainment. Yup, it's the **National Western Stock Show and Rodeo.** Eighty years ago, cowboys' competitions with each other were formalized into rodeos in a circus tent in 1906; the high speed of the riders, the antics of the rodeo clowns and the sweet smells of the animals sometimes still remind you of a circus. For 11 days every January, old Buffalo Bill and his Wild West entertainers seem to return to old Denver Town.

The National Western remains an important stock show, too.

You can view more than 20,000 live, scrubbed and brushed Herefords, Angus, Simmentals, Shorthorns, Longhorns, Arabian horses, Morgan horses, draft horses, miniature horses, ewes and lambs, all in their neat pens. You watch shearing contests, breeding cattle auctions, the judging of quarter horse stallions. Some 400,000 visitors flock to the arenas to buy, sell, learn, socialize. Millions of dollars change hands here.

"This is a cowboy convention for real-life cowboys," says one longtime Stock Show regular. "It's big business for the people who grow the stuff that ends up in our refrigerators and stomachs."

In addition to the judging and auctions, there are lectures, sales booths, meetings and contests for the cattlemen and women who show up here. Lots of money is in evidence. Thousand dollar alligator boots. Hundred dollar Stetsons. Belt buckles with diamonds. Even silver halters for the horses. A big commerce in livestock supplies, raw wool, saddles, cow tags, Western oil paintings, lassoes.

New techniques are taught in feeding and breeding. In the arenas, you see riding demonstrations by horsewomen who gallop at a breakneck pace. Red-vested auctioneers and a peopled tribune asplash in color pays attention to a sale of—yes!—*llamas* from South America. A children's area delights the young ones with displays of baby rabbits, geese, piglets. Each day some 6,000 school children are bused here to see the animals. The multifaceted spectacular not only brings aristocratic purebred livestock to Denver. The Stock Show regularly attracts the best of the rodeo ring, all top contenders for national championships for female barrel-racing, calf roping, bull and bronco riding, steer wrestling and many more events by the 1,100 professional rodeo cowboys and cowgirls who are courageous and sporty. More than $400,000 in prizes are at stake.

But not all cowboys do well in Denver. A horse may refuse to buck and the rider will get nothing. A horse tosses him off after two seconds and the rider will get nothing. "They're the great American gamblers on horseback," says a Western radio announcer.

Rodeo riders may be among the last American heroes or heroines. It takes nerve to tackle a furious, crowd-crazed animal and stay on it for eight seconds. It takes true guts to look injury in the eye without flinching.

Nobody gives the competitors an expense account. They pay their own way to ride at the National Western Stock Show. The rodeo cowboy draws no allowance, has no guaranteed annual wage. The only income comes from earnings in a fiercely competitive sport where he must win not only against other men, but against the "rank" (mean) animals. And he must pay for this privilege—entry fees that can run into several hundred dollars per event per rodeo.

The excitement of barrel racing in Denver

Most riders hail from small towns and made their first acquaintance with horses as kids. One typical bareback champ comes from Cora, Wyoming. He started as a ranch hand.

Rodeos, such as the National Western in Denver, may have well begun as a prank, a diversion for ranch hands, cowpokes. A few specialists, the "roughstring" riders who busted wild horses for a livelihood at $3 to $5 apiece were quick to show their stuff. They were a tough bunch of men. Hardened by the summer heat and the winter blizzards. Used to riding through long nights. They had to deal with stampeding herds, crippled animals and cattle rustlers. Their horses were extensions of themselves. They lived in the saddle.

Rodeo must have started during the early cattle drives and on the scattered ranches. A historian of the Denver-based Professional Rodeo Cowboys Association explains: "When their work was done, the cowboys entertained each other with roping and riding contests, showing off the skills they had sharpened during their everyday work on the range."

In the early 1880s, American ranchers began to develop the "ranch show" as a spectator sport. Already in 1888, Colorado spectators paid money to watch cowboys on bucking broncs. Within 20 years these affairs had become known as rodeos and were drawing crowds on tour in the cities of the United States.

In the early days of rodeo, the rider stayed in the saddle "until the horse was rode or the cowboy throwed." Today, the saddle bronc rider must stay aboard eight seconds while at the same time not disqualifying himself in any number of ways. A man has to zoom out of the chute with both feet in the stirrups.

As a spectator, you can see lots of thrilling action, all the while being seated comfortably in the **Denver Coliseum.** The Stock Show grounds sprawl across 150 acres, which are only about 100 yards south of I-70. Buses get you there all day long; free shuttles run from various downtown hotels. You can also take a cab or drive. In that case, keep in mind that thousands of visiting livestock folks and rodeo fans compete for room to leave their cars, so close-in parking isn't always plentiful.

Rodeo competition takes place both afternoons and evenings. Tickets cost no more than for a movie. But wait! Have you ever been to a motion picture where you could witness a llama auction, an Australian-style sheep-shearing contest, the world's largest bull show (with one animal actually selling at $300,000), a catch-a-calf competition for teenagers? What film lets you talk to a real, true-blue Colorado rancher?

National Western Stock Show and Rodeo, 1325 East Forty-Sixth Avenue, Denver, CO 80216; (303) 297-1166.

Buckhorn Exchange
Restaurant and Museum

How would you like to dine in a historic landmark and museum? How about a steaming platter of elk steak at a table under a stuffed elk or a plate heaped with buffalo meat, with mounted buffaloes staring down? The **Buckhorn Exchange** is allegedly Colorado's oldest restaurant. It is certainly one of the most original. Moreover, it's a saloon, a singles bar, a magnet for celebrities and tourists and a moneymaker.

Supper here appeals to well-heeled meat eaters: 24-ounce T-bone steaks, 14-ounce New York steaks, buffaloes kabob, pork chops, Rocky Mountain oysters, rabbit—all at hefty deluxe rates in a noisy congenial atmosphere. The saloon is upstairs, complete with a giant oak bar that was shipped here by ox cart. Nearby walls are filled with 1902 photos of hunting parties; even the men's room has historical pictures of stagecoaches.

The downstairs restaurant-museum is cluttered with more than 500 taxidermy pieces including antelopes, deer, bear, wolverine, mountain goats, moose, weasels, zebra, birds of all kinds,

Buckhorn Restaurant & Museum

shapes and plumage. You can look at more than a hundred rifles, pistols and other weapons. You dine at 110-year-old poker tables covered with cozy red-checkered tablecloths. There's lunch, too, if you want it, with good pot roast, a Buckhorn dip, bratwurst or the specialty of the house, a navy bean soup. Lunch is popular with the downtown Yuppie business crowd; dinner attracts out-of-towners that include many Europeans. Europe can never match the Buckhorn's true-blue American West.

Even the restaurant's history has its fascinating aspects. It was begun in 1893 by owner Henry H. Zietz, a cowboy and scout with Buffalo Bill, no less, personal bodyguard of Leadville's silver millionaire H. A. W. Horace Tabor and hunting guide of President Teddy Roosevelt, who actually arrived in his private train in front of the Buckhorn. The restaurant's official history relates that Henry Zietz "catered to cattlemen, miners, railroad builders, Indian chiefs, silver barons, roustabouts, gamblers, the great and the near-great." In December, 1900, a masked gunman rode up to the restaurant, waved a .45, and demanded all money and valuables to be placed on the bar, "and be quick about it!" The fellow's horse had been tied to the Buckhorn's hitching post, but when the gunman rode away at a gallop, he found himself pursued by Zietz' rifle-raising customers, who "handily dispatched the miscreant to greener pastures."

After the Zietz family's death, the restaurant-museum passed into the capable hands of two Denver real estate tycoons, Roi Davis and Steve Knowlton, who put large sums into restoring the building and its contents in 1978. They also raised the prices to twentieth-century levels. The Buckhorn is in the National Register of Historic Places by order of the Department of the Interior.

A meal here will delight Texans and other travelers from all over the world.

The Buckhorn's red brick building is easy to find at 1000 Osage Street, Denver, CO 80204. More details? The location is between Colfax Avenue and Eighth Avenue, west of Santa Fe Street.

The Buckhorn Exchange is open for lunch (expensive) Monday through Friday from 11 a.m.–3 p.m., and dinner is served seven nights a week, starting at 5 p.m. (deluxe). Reservations suggested. (303) 534-9505.

Larimer Square

Larimer Square is a renovated eighteenth-century downtown oasis with a national reputation; indeed, it is the second most visited landmark in Colorado. (The Air Force Academy is the first).

The area fetches a lot of people—especially in the afternoons and evenings and on weekends. As you step in and out of the red brick courtyards, walk under arches and peek into shops (that are sometimes flanked by flower vendors), you are apt to mingle with groups of well-behaved teenagers, a young out-of-town crowd, flight attendants, Nebraska farm girls, local junior executives. Foreign visitors are delighted with the history of Larimer Square, the stories of miners and goldseekers.

In 1858 Gen. William E. Larimer erected Denver's first building here. It was a mere log cabin. More than one hundred years later, a group of Colorado business people founded the Larimer Square Association for the purpose of restoring the old buildings. The excitement that once was historic Larimer Street soon returned in the form of promenades, carriage rides and quaint shops between Fourteenth and Fifteenth streets.

While the area might be small, it is a concentration of interesting restaurants, cafes, chic boutiques and stores that deserve special attention. The merchandise here is invariably smart and interesting, the prices slightly higher than at stores

Return to Victorian elegance at Larimer Square, a restored section of Denver's oldest street. Shops, restaurants and nightclubs are housed in turn-of-the-century buildings.

in the average shopping center. The mood in the shops is mellow and low pressure, a feeling enhanced by occasional outdoor chamber musicians during the summer.

The Square should be a good shopping choice for guests in downtown hotels. It is easy to reach on foot; if you don't like to walk, you can take the free shuttles that race along the **Sixteenth Street Mall** to Larimer. The restored shopping and dining quarter, as well as most of downtown Denver, is well policed and safe for folks of all ages—even in the evening.

Larimer Square frequently features events that highlight the city's cosmopolitan aspects. In the past, an **International Spring Fest** took place here, with wines and foods of many countries. Periodically, Colorado's fruit and vegetable farmers set up a market. A **Mexican Fiesta**, a genuine beer and *wurst* German **Oktober-Fest** are held. At Christmas, the street is prettily decorated and Denverites come for special festivities, listening to choirs and carolers, and enjoying a myriad of Christmas lights.

In some ways Larimer Square reminds you of Ghirardelli

Square in San Francisco. Or it may make you think of Greenwich Village or New Orleans's French Quarter; others compare it to Chicago's Old Town or Toronto's Yorktown. By the same token, Larimer Square has its own visual personality; it remains an outstanding example of early Denver Victorian architecture complete with gas lights, handwrought lead windows, stairways, historic markers, restored cornices, handsome outdoor benches for resting and watching. In the restaurants (pricey) and shops, you find Tiffany lamps, cherrywood bars, rosewood paneling, old wallpapers and lead ceilings.

The Square is paved with the legends of the nineteenth century.

Larimer Street in Denver was once the most famous thoroughfare in the West. The restaurants, hotels and theatres of its heyday were renowned. Stories of what happened when the greats, near-greats and desperados of the West made good newspaper copy. And tales of what went on behind closed doors in the neighborhood shocked a nation. Gambling and boozing were rampant.

Named for Denver's founder, Gen. William E. Larimer, the street played a prominent role in the city's political and commercial history from Nov. 16, 1858. That first day, Denver City consisted only of Larimer Street's 1400 block. As the western town grew around it, the original site became Denver's first commercial and governmental center. Here were the first post office, the first departmnet store, the first drugstore, the first bank and government buildings of the 1860s, 70s and 80s.

As the years passed, Denver gradually moved uptown and Larimer Street became a skid row area. Thanks to the gin mills and flophouses, the handsome Victorian buildings were forgotten, although amid the grime and dirt, their architectural beauty remained. Razing was a frequent threat.

It took an energetic woman, Dana Crawford, to find the investors and obtain help from the city fathers, to bring urban renewal and the rebirth of history to Larimer Square. It is now a Landmark Preservation District. You find this important Denver tourist attraction listed in the National Register of Historic Places.

The two-block Larimer Street area between Fourteenth and Fifteenth streets is easily reached on foot or by free shuttle from Denver's downtown hotels. For information: (303) 534-2367.

Museum of Western Art

Do you know a museum devoted exclusively to Western art? Such museums are scarce indeed. And there is no better way to bring the frontier alive than through name painters—the great ones such as Albert Bierstadt, Karl Bodmer, Thomas Moran, Charles Russell, Thomas Hart Benton, Ernest Blumenschein or through the action-packed bronze statues of Frederic Remington. These are hallowed art names—many from the last century—artists who still knew how to *draw* or paint traditional oils or watercolors (unlike some contemporaries who are only able to splash color on a canvas or use the ruler for straight minimalist lines).

Denver's **Museum of Western Art** opened in 1983. A Colorado governor spoke of it glowingly as "providing a missing link." Denverites and visitors have paid homage to the chronologically arranged art. Its themes fit perfectly into Colorado and frontier history: rousing scenes of trappers facing bears, buffalo hunts, cattle roundups, Indian flights, attacks on trains or stagecoaches, canyonlands, waterfalls and magnificent mountains. Each canvas or watercolor reflects artistic integrity and perfect control of the medium—rare qualities indeed.

The building that houses the collection sits across from the famous Brown Palace Hotel. The museum was well designed as a mix of renovation and restoration, complete with a bookstore in the basement. One area is reserved for special exhibitions such as Thomas Moran's well-known Yellowstone illustrations, produced on location during a 1871 expedition. The 125 or so paintings—and the existence of the Denver-based museum—all came together through the efforts of William Foxley, a Montana cattleman and entrepreneur. It was Foxley who sought out the many owners and collectors of the Remingtons, Russells, Bierstadts and many more. The acquisition of these art works proved to be a difficult task, as was finding a site and getting assistance from the Colorado Senate.

Even before the museum's inauguration in 1983, the Victorian building itself had an interesting history. The site at 1727 Tremont Place started as a school that taught "Christian virtues" to young ladies. After the building owner's death a few years later, the school took on a new life as Hotel Richelieu and finally the Navarre. Ironically, these were gambling and sex establishments for the nouveau riches of the West. In 1892, an underground tunnel began to link the Navarre with the Brown

Palace—which became a discreet passageway to the brothel and gaming activities. In 1904, the address was turned into a fine restaurant, which continued business under various managements until 1977. William Foxley's efforts followed. The building is listed in the National Register of Historic Places.

The Museum of Western Art depends on the modest admission fee and on contributions plus memberships. The location is 1727 Tremont Place; the phone (303) 296-1880. Visiting hours: Tuesday through Saturday 10 a.m.–4:30 p.m.

The Brown Palace Hotel

From its international debut in 1892 until the present, Denver's **Brown Palace Hotel** has lived up to its motto, "Where the World Registers." Indeed, this historic hotel is a classic. Celebrities and royalty have graced its corridors. Katharine Hepburn, Bob Hope, Molly Brown, the Beatles, King Hussein of Jordan and every United States president since Theodore Roosevelt have left their signatures in the guest book.

The Brown, as Denverites have nicknamed it, is a remarkable example of Victorian architecture. The hotel lobby impresses the most. Upon entering, your eyes look up the six tiers of wrought iron balconies to the stained glass cathedral ceiling. The decorative stone beneath your feet is Mexican onyx. Changing displays of historical memorabilia decorate the luxurious lobby. Old guest registers, menus and photographs take you back to relive the role the Brown Palace played in the history of Denver.

The hotel is named for its builder, Henry Cordes Brown. As Brown watched nineteenth-century Denver grow, he saw the need of a fine hostelry for visiting easterners who came to do business with Colorado mining companies and railroads. The builder envisioned this fine edifice to rise from a triangular plot of land he owned near the center of the city. Henry Cordes Brown examined and studied the blueprints of the world's deluxe hotels before he developed his "palace."

A prominent Denver architect, Frank E. Edbrooke, designed a building in the spirit of the Italian Renaissance. Because of the geometric pattern of Brown's land, the hotel took on an unusual shape. Edbrooke gave the building a trio-frontage and then planned it so each room faced a street. Without any interior rooms, every guest could have a view, plus morning or afternoon sunshine! The contractors, Geddes and Serrie, constructed this

Famous Brown Palace Hotel in downtown Denver

soon-to-be famous landmark from Colorado red granite and warm brown Arizona sandstone. James Whitehouse then carved a lovely series of medallions in the stone.

Completed in 1892, the ten-story building had 400 rooms. Fireplaces were standard for each room as well as bathroom taps yielding artesian water straight from the hotel's wells (as they still do today). The finest achievements in steam heating and electricity were incorporated into the structure. The Brown was also noted as the second fireproof edifice in the country.

It took four years and $1,600,000 to complete Henry Brown's luxurious dream. Cool water flowed from the taps; steam heat provided warmth. Ice machines kept the wine chilled and the produce fresh. Turkish Baths, hairdressing parlors, billiard rooms—even a hotel library!—were available for guest use. Linens, china, glassware and silver came from the finest craftsmen. Carpets and curtains in each room had special designs. Excellence abounded at every turn.

The Brown Palace opened for a banquet of the Triennial

Conclave of Knights Templar and their ladies. A seven-course dinner at $10 a plate was served in the main dining room on the eighth floor. The guests viewed over 300 miles of Rocky Mountain grandeur from the wide dining room windows.

Denver society was formally introduced to the Brown Palace a few months later when the Tabors threw a fancy ball. In the years since, the Brown has hosted thousands of such glittering evenings.

Today, the Brown Palace Hotel is listed in the National Register of Historic Places. Even in the midst of modern times, it continues to provide guests with historical authenticity, Victorian charm and good service. The original decor has been preserved, especially in the restaurants—the hallmarks of the hotel.

The **Ship's Tavern** is an exceptionally handsome room where you can find a measure of peace in a pub-like, comfortable atmosphere created by antiques, old sailing ships and checkered tablecloths. This distinguished Brown Palace eatery is a good spot for a late sandwich, a prime rib dinner or good drinks. The Ship's Tavern, (303) 825-3111, is open every day of the year. Highly recommended for late hours and a nightcap but not for lunch, when things get hectic (expensive).

In **Ellyngton's Restaurant**, you're reminded of the first-class aboard one of those old transatlantic liners. The people are wealthy—local lawyers, stockbrokers, physicians, tycoons and the well-to-do shopkeepers. The mood is genteel, slightly old-fashioned, relaxing and the average age always seems to hover between 35 and 75. Many people come for dinner, which is taken at exceptionally spacious round, white-clothed tables. Other visitors merely arrive for a *creme de menthe*.

The Brown's burgundy-colored **Palace Arms** room is decorated with ancient flags, Napoleonic relics and fine etchings. The expert service by uniformed waiters with gold-braid epaulettes and the attentive old maitre d's are all easy to take. Unlike so many of Denver's dining places, the Palace Arms provides good lighting; each table has its own lamp. A Brown Palace brochure quotes the late Lucius Beebe, one of the longtime regulars, who praised the bill of fare. "It is notable," commented Beebe, "that the menu doesn't contain the word 'epicure,' nor are the dishes advertised with lyric adjectives."

Indeed, the Palace Arms food is straighforward; it emphasizes beef and lamb. You know that you're at a good restaurant, however, when the waiter respects your time limits; he brings the assorted luncheon dishes without those hour-long pauses that can kill a person's hunger, or your next appointment.

On Friday and Saturday nights, the Brown Palace offers dancing to the sounds of a live Big Band orchestra. This 1940s attraction continues as a regular weekend feature in Ellyngton's, the hotel's main dining room. It's a special place to enjoy sumptuous fares. (The tariff ranges from expensive to deluxe, depending on the dishes.)

In the last few years a new wing and a **Grand Ballroom** have been added. In the rooms the furnishings range from elegant period pieces to striking modern. Everything has been well planned by interior decorators. No two suites in the hotel are alike; the shape, size and decor of each reflects a different historic period. The Eisenhower Suite, for example, served as summer headquarters for Dwight and Mamie Eisenhower during one presidential campaign. Containing a piano and chaise lounge, it is decorated according to Mamie's taste. Suite 840 has a gate of golden rings opening to a private hallway. Elaborate chandeliers and mirrored ceilings highlight these rooms.

Conveniently located at Seventeenth and Tremont, the Brown Palace Hotel is in the heart of downtown Denver's financial and shopping district. Many sights and cultural points of interest are within walking distance. It pays to make reservations two weeks in advance. Phone: (303) 297-3111.

Denver, Colorado — also lots of lovely parks . . .

Denver's Parks with Charisma

Washington Park—my favorite—on a late September morning. One of Colorado's poet laureates, at age 90, likes to walk around one of the lakes here. But he's nowhere in sight at this after-breakfast hour. Actually, it has started to snow. Winter without the benefit of fall. Yesterday, the sun still blazed here and now the flakes tumble thickly. The lake steams.

Normally filled with cyclists, the park is deserted. Denver's polluted air is being washed clean by the moisture. A few hardy joggers, wool caps over their ears, jog along the lake paths. The grass is still too warm for the snow to stick; the wet meadows seem greener than any time of the year.

The miniblizzard stops. Clouds drift overhead.

Through the park you can see some of Denver's old homes on Downing, Louisiana and Franklin streets. Typically, all the houses come with lawns and gardens. The latter form the visitor's first impressions.

And the parks!

The city of Denver boasts over one hundred named parks of various sizes and shapes that stretch in every direction. It is said to be America's largest such system. Green areas abound. If you visit the Denver **Civic Center**, for instance, you'll at once notice the many well-tended lawns and trees. Not far away, you see the gold-domed **State Capitol.** Step into the marbled and onyxed halls and look at the paintings of pioneer scenes. Study the legends. "And men shall fashion glaciers into greenness and harvest April rivers in the autumn," reads one poetic caption.

It captures the citizens' fondness for their greenery. Each year, Denverites go in for lawn contests (who has the prettiest one?). Every day, the newspapers print advice on lawn care. A wail goes up if a city father hints at the possibility of rationing the water used for sprinklers. Stores keep large stocks of fertilizer, and commerce is brisk in garden tools, boxes of petunias and geraniums that embellish the most humble Denver gardens.

On weekends, Denverites repair to their public parks, which must be among the most well-kept and varied in the nation. Each of the city's parks has its own charisma, its own subtle characteristics depending on location, size and activities.

Begin with Denver's largest, **City Park.** You reach it from downtown in ten minutes of driving (enter the gates at East

Twentieth Avenue and York Street). Keep in mind that you could spend a full summer day and evening here without a moment's boredom.

A family may while away many hours, for instance, in the zoo. Hundreds of animals frolic or loaf on some 70 acres of grounds. Take the children to Monkey Island, where monkeys swing and leap all summer (in spring you'll find these critters still in the Primate House). A special glass edifice contains dozens of colorful chirping, singing, talking birds. Other natural habitat areas are for polar bears, llamas, turtles, baby elephants, rhinos, giraffes, 1,500 animals in all. A special zoo for small children is popular; here you find young ducks, lambs, chickens and other farm animals. The zoo is open from 10 a.m.–5 p.m.

Active youngsters—and exercise-seeking adults—will welcome City Park's large lake, with its many paddleboats that work like bicycles. A small train circles a lagoon and crosses tiny trestled bridges with a view of assorted geese and swans.

City Park has considerable tennis action, too. Fifteen hard-surface courts are always available gratis on a first-come-first-served basis. Denverites of all ages sometimes compete in local tournaments here.

PHOTO BY HELEN EVANS

Washington Park in Denver is one of the city's most attractive

City Park also has an adjacent 18-hole municipal golf course. (Entrance at East Twenty-Fifth Avenue and York Street.) A tourist may rent equipment and carts at modest fees.

The park is ideal for the economy-minded. One can feed ducks at a small lake, take long walks on clean paths, and watch the children on myriad playgrounds. Bear in mind that in good weather—and Denver weather is mostly sunny in summer and fall—you also have access to softball courts and to bicycle trails, the latter around the pleasant lake.

A weekday may be the best day to stroll through Denver's **Washington Park**, at S. Downing and E. Virginia streets, not far from E. Alameda Avenue. The wide expanse of green is almost unknown to tourists, despite all the delights here: small creeks are shaded by willows and cottonwoods. Anything and everything happens at Washington Park on weekends; young lovers from nearby Denver University walk along the paths; the poet laureate walks his dog; elderly gentlemen play a game of *boccie* in slow motion on a special well-kept lawn; young champions slam tennis balls across one of the many free courts; an entire family feeds ducks and geese. Washington Park has

Denver's many parks include this one on Sloan's Lake

PHOTO BY CURTIS W. CASEWIT

several playgrounds for small-fry, and plenty of picnic tables. Washington Park comes with ample flowerbeds that remind you of English gardens.

The park also boasts a large recreation center where you can swim indoors, work out in a gym with sophisticated machinery, join a basketball game, or, if you stay in town long enough, take various classes that range from puppetry to pottery. The modernistic recreation center is ideal for rainy days.

Happiness for Denverites is **Sloan's Lake,** located between Sheridan Boulevard and Newton. The lakeshore and the grass fetch an elderly clientele, pensioners, retired railroad people, young Vietnamese, old Indians, some fishing out of their automobiles, others sitting near the water.

No crowds during the week. Then on summer Saturdays, a crescendo of people. The climax comes on July Sundays or holidays. From July 4th to Labor Day, the parking lots cannot hold all the automobiles with picnickers and their baskets, with more anglers hoping for a ten-pound carp, teenagers ready to toss footballs, baseballs, plastic platters, ladies with grandchildren, three-year-olds waving bags of bread. Orange-beaked ducks waddle eagerly ashore; wild Canada geese float with nonchalance toward the toss of popcorn.

You see father and son teams playing—surprise!—a game of croquet; you see water-skiers in black wet suits. Windy days produce sailboats—30 of them—50?—a regatta!—sailors— plying the blue Sloan's Lake surface in their dinghies, Snipes or Sunfish vessels. The joggers are always in evidence, too, and in any weather, a few old, sometimes overweight couples walk around the lake—doctor's orders. On sunny days, the Rockies wink in the background.

You can enter the Park from W. Seventeenth Avenue or from Sheridan Boulevard and from several other points, all west of Federal Boulevard and south of West Colfax Avenue.

Cheesman Park, between E. Twelfth and E. Eighth (and Franklin Street) is small, but takes pride in its many well-kept flowers. Denverites are generous with their green areas: you may sit on the grass any time. This city oasis comes with outdoor tables and a small, elevated templelike stone edifice that affords an excellent view of the mountains. Denver's **Botanic Gardens** (at 909 York Street) are close to Cheesman Park.

The late Vladimir Golschmann, symphony conductor, had an apartment overlooking these green acres. Almost every

Denver's many parks include CHEESMAN PARK, with this Greek edifice

Denver morning, he'd step to his balcony. "I come out here and I feel I'm part of the landscape," Golschmann once told a friend. "Where else can you have this wonderful feeling?"

Actually, Denver's municipal parks stimulate plenty of outdoor life on 2,800 acres; to these, you may add another city-owned 14,000 acres in the foothills. Wildflowers! Spruce trees! Pines! Meadows!

Small wonder that Denver is called "The City of Green."

Farm Country

"Colorado? Ah, high peaks! Mountain towns! Skiing!" This is how many easterners, southerners and midwesterners describe their idea of a state that has mountains on its license plates. Even Europeans know about the Rockies. The plains—especially Colorado's eastern plains, the farmer's domain!—come as a surprise.

Yet much of the land belongs to agriculture. As you drive east from Denver, Colorado Springs, Pueblo, Trinidad, the country takes on the flat character of Kansas and Nebraska, with which Colorado shares its eastern border. The names turn rural: Punkin Center. Wild Horse. Deer Trail.

Communities like Wray, Holyoke or Yuma all got their start through homesteading. About 94 percent of Colorado's land consists of dry or irrigated farmlands, rangeland and forests.

Eastern Colorado was first settled during the mid and late 1880s. Little agricultural communities like Haxtun, Kiowa, Eads sprang up. Oats, barley, wheat and corn were planted; harvesting was done with primitive machinery. Some of the farms were the result of the early railroads selling cheap tracts of land to the immigrants.

The homesteaders fought hard financial battles when the droughts hit in 1890. But the Homestead Act, which presented volunteer farmers with 160 free acres, was a big incentive in Colorado. Many of the settlers demanded few luxuries from their homesteads. They tilled, planted, harvested, faced blizzards and hailstorms, grasshoppers and more droughts. The worst ones hit during the 1930s. Still, through the years, eastern Colorado produced not just corn and wheat but also dry beans, alfafa, potatoes, onions, rye, sorghum and commercial vegetables. In Rocky Ford, year after year, the citizens grew watermelons and cantaloupes.

The farmers endured the summer heat and dust storms. World War II was good to the Colorado farm economy. New well-drilling techniques and irrigation improved the situation. During the 1960s, wheat sales hit record figures. The 1970s brought prosperity. The export trade flourished. Land prices soared. Farmers splurged on newfangled $100,000 machinery.

When exports shrunk, as everywhere in the Midwest and West, the Colorado farmers suffered. The 1980s have been harsh to the eastern part of the state. Prices dropped for crops while everything else costs more.

Yet some farmers survive. A few lucky ones—close to cities like Denver, Fort Morgan, Sterling—switched to sod farming.

They create instant lawns for suburbia, as an adjunct to the housing explosion. Near Parker you see miles and miles of green carpets, well-watered, neatly rolled up, ready for shipment. New homes still go up in Englewood, Littleton, Aurora, Thornton, Castle Rock, and each house clamors for its swath of green, often supplied by sod farmers.

Others stay on and grow "Hard Red" winter wheat and specialty items like asparagus, flowers, peas, sunflower seeds. A small number build greenhouses or mushroom cellars. Dry beans and millet bring profits.

Others go bankrupt, or seek jobs in the city. Third-generation farmers sometimes give up; regretfully, their children move to town. Some are lucky enough to sell their land to developers of condos and shopping centers. One well-known dairy farmer plans to develop himself. Farmers turn into land managers for absentee agribusiness owners. The Colorado farm wives, meanwhile, try to hold the marriages together. If they're lucky, they can still see their men out there, in the field under the open sky, working from dusk to dawn.

For the Colorado farmers who can hang on to their house and their soil, life can still be good. They know about city crime only from hearsay or their TV sets. Child molestation is rare. Rape is nearly unknown in places like Wray (pop. 2,100) or Eads (900) and many others. The cowardly Denver muggers and stickup men of 7-11's don't show up in the hamlets of eastern Colorado where the sheriff and State Patrol could catch them right quick. The bank robbers, professional burglars and other rifraff stay in the metropolis; they seldom venture into farm country.

The scenery packs little excitement. Abandoned houses, an occasional silo and fields in all directions. Grain elevator. Weighing station. Plows holding court. Small communities where one automatically slows down for the sights of feed stores or an old 12-unit motel, or the cafe with home cooking. Many of the little hamlets in eastern Colorado seem alike. Small houses with porches. Shop windows with tools, placed there helter-skelter. After nine at night, almost everything is closed. Main Street is so silent that you can hear the crickets in the field.

Each little town has several churches, which get busy on Sunday. Sermons on your car radio. A quick glance through a picture window shows a farmer watching a television evangelist. Does the preacher have an answer when the banks want their money? Or the man's farm is to be auctioned off to his creditors next week?

The inhabitants of eastern Colorado are reserved, not too friendly, perhaps distrustful, certainly preoccupied. But they have time. "Oh, sure," says one of them to an inquirer from the city. "Sure, we have problems. But there's more space to have them in."

Northeastern Colorado

Most visitors—and even new immigrants to Colorado—think the state consists mostly of Denver and suburbs, and perhaps a few mountain towns like Vail and Aspen. They often forget northern and northeastern Colorado. When Mark Twain visited in 1862, however, he reveled in the prairie and the horses. "It was a noble sport gallopping over the plain in the dewy freshness of the morning," Twain wrote.

The dewy freshness is still there, along with the star-filled sky, some farms with their tilled fields, the big cottonwoods. Despite the giant interstate highways, the air is still pure. Unlike in Denver, where the car-caused pollution backs up against the mountains, the breezes from the northwest do a fine purification job. The cities of Fort Collins, Greeley and Longmont have expanded; luckily, however, there is very little smokestack industry. You see new shopping malls and Holiday Inns and Kentucky Fried Chicken outposts. The tourists flock to communities such as Loveland, with its lakes and access to the Rocky Mountain National Park.

In the same region, **Fort Collins** may well be the most sophisticated community in northern Colorado. With 65,000 inhabitants, it is the largest. Hordes of eager, serious **Colorado State University** students are here, and the visitor quickly becomes aware of wider interests: Fort Collins has several bookstores, numerous foreign car dealers and shops catering to the young. The distance to Denver is a manageable 66 miles.

Much of Colorado's famous corn-fed beef comes from Fort Collins. The dry climate is ideal for the Hereford and Angus cattle, and northern Colorado cattle feeders have worked out precise feeding systems. From this region, the aged beef is shipped all over the world.

In recent years, the area's ranchers have adapted themselves to the times. They now raise calves that are leaner and less cholesterol-laden. Low-fat feeding methods are in. Marbled meat is out. Moreover, some of these contemporary cattlemen shun growth stimulants and avoid antibiotics.

The Fort Collins-based Colorado State University is strong on agriculture and also trains forestry students whose tree nurseries one can visit. The city has its own symphony orchestra and a theatre. "We're often underestimated," says one Fort Collins official. "We shouldn't be. We're a microcosm of Denver, but without the air pollution and crime."

Just south is **Loveland**, only half the size of Fort Collins, yet it has carved a national name for itself. Loveland calls itself "Colorado's Sweetheart City."

Each year, many sacks of valentines are being remailed here;

the sentimental souls who send these love messages are backed by the town's civic leaders who volunteer their time. Tradition! Cupid has worked here for some four decades. Loveland's postmasters themselves often create the corny poems that appear in cachet form next to the Loveland stamp. A typical verse:

> The day is full of gladness
> And eyes with stardust shine
> When Cupid works his magic
> In this lovely valentine.

The Loveland post office patiently copes with the extra work of some 400,000 valentines with the blessing of the town officials. Local high schools paint heart signs. On the Chamber of Commerce maps Loveland appears in the shape of a heart, and the yearly "Miss Valentine" wears hearts on her apron. The local business community has no objections; there are now even a **Sweetheart Shops** and **Sweetheart Lanes.** Ironically, Loveland was named after a railroad robber baron.

Actually, agriculture and tourism go on strongly here, too: you spot cornfields and sugar beets, ride horses at local stables, use local campgrounds and visit the numerous Loveland recreation areas. And the thousands of valentines via "Cupid's Hometown" or "the Valentine Capital of the World" are a business by themselves.

The city of **Greeley** (founded by Horace Greeley, the newspaper publisher) is a few miles to the east of Loveland. Greeley was meant to become an agricultural colony, too, and succeeded. All around the town's perimeter, you see sugar beet fields, barley and other crops.

Much of the local sightseeing harks back to agriculture. At the (summer only) **Centennial Village**, the curators erected a sod house, a homesteader's wagon house and a one-room rural school. The **Greeley Public Library** displays photos of assorted ethnic immigrant farm families. Rodeos are popular and Greeley's annual **Weld Fair,** has livestock shows complete with poultry, rabbits, sheep and displays of various field crops.

To be sure, James Michener was inspired to write his bestselling novel *Centennial* through his familiarity and on-location research in Greeley and surroundings.

Michener's fictional pioneers built their town of Centennial on the Platte River. The story is one of struggle, success, failure and, above all, endurance. Perhaps the closest thing to his invented Centennial is the near-ghost town of **Keota**, Colorado, 40 miles northeast of Greeley. Michener returned to Keota more than a dozen times to absorb its atmosphere and talk with postmaster Clyde Stanley.

Stanley had lived in Keota most of his 70 years. He had seen the eager farmers come, only to be displaced by drought and dust storms. He watched the town dwindle from 129 people in 1929 to 6 in 1970. Michener dedicated the book to Stanley, "who introduced me to the prairie."

Not many people—or even Michener's readers—realize that the famous author had good reasons to turn to Greeley and northwestern Colorado for his research. In 1936, at the age of 29 and not yet a writer, Michener taught in Greeley at what was to become the **University of North Colorado.**

He never regretted his decision. "In Greeley, I grew up spiritually, emotionally, intellectually," he later noted in John P. Hayes's *James A. Michener: A Biography.*

While there, Michener became friends with Floyd Merrill, Greeley's newspaper editor. The pair made almost weekly ventures into the surrounding country. At least three times a month, Merrill and the future bestselling author took off for

PHOTO BY HELEN EVANS

Author hiking in Denver foothills

exploration to the intricate irrigation systems that produced Colorado's vegetables and fruit, sometimes to the mountains. "We would look down into valleys crowded with blue spruce and aspen, and quite often out onto the prairie east of town where majestic buttes rose starkly from the barren waste," Michener relates in Hayes's biography.

Merrill also taught the young professor to use a camera. Michener credits the photos he took in Colorado with keeping his images of the West alive and vital long enough for *Centennial* to be conceived.

Already famous in 1970, the author returned to Colorado, determined to write an exhaustive story of the Western experience. He explored the natural and social history of the region.

And he made Northeastern Colorado famous.

INDEX

Off The Beaten Path in . . .

Also of interest from THE GLOBE PEQUOT PRESS:

The "Guide to the Recommended Country Inns" series
New England • Mid-Atlantic States and Chesapeake Region • South
Midwest • West Coast • Rocky Mountain Region • Arizona   New Mexico,
and Texas.

Historic Country House Hotels: Great Britain & Ireland
The Best Pubs of Great Britain
The Best Bed & Breakfast in the World: United Kingdom
Guide to Eastern Canada
Guide to Western Canada
Guide to the National Park Areas: Eastern States
Guide to the National Park Areas: Western States
Daytrips and Budget Vacations in New England
Daytrips, Getaway Weekends, and Budget Vacations in the Mid-Atlantic States
Historic Walks in Old Boston
Historic Walks in Cambridge
In and Out of Boston with (or without) Children
The California Bed & Breakfast Book
Bed & Breakfast in the Caribbean
America's Grand Resort Hotels
Home Exchanging: A Complete Sourcebook for Travelers at Home or Abroad

"Off the Beaten Path" series
Colorado • New York • Illinois • Indiana • Ohio • Virginia • Florida

Day Trips from Baltimore
Day Trips from Houston
Day Trips from Cincinnati
Day Trips from Phoenix, Tucson, and Flagstaff
Train Trips: Exploring America by Rail/revised edition, includes Canada
The Jersey Shore: A Travel and Pleasure Guide
The Grand Strand: An Uncommon Guide to Myrtle Beach and Its
    Surroundings
Blue Ridge Mountain Pleasures
Walking from Inn to Inn: The San Francisco Bay Area
Hiking from Inn to Inn: Wilderness Walking Tours with Comfortable
    Overnight Lodging from Maine to Virginia
What to Do with the Kids This Year: One Hundred Family Vacation Places
    with Time Off for You!

**Available at your bookstore or direct from the publisher. For a free catalogue
or to place an order, call 1-800-243-0495 (in Connecticut, call 1-800-962-0973)
or write to The Globe Pequot Press, 138 West Main Street, Box Q, Chester,
Connecticut 06412.**